Cognitive Cardio

Puzzles for a Healthy Heart & Mind

Pass the time, stimulate your brain, and learn more about your heart health during cardiac recovery

To Mark
wishing you health, wealth and happiness
Sallie xXx

SALLIE CRAWLEY

The information contained within this book is for general information purpose only. It is not official health advice and is not intended to be used as such.

Any action you take upon the information you find in this book is strictly at your own risk.

Any material or information in this book is not medical or therapeutic and is not intended to diagnose, treat, cure or prevent any medical condition or disease.

If you have any questions pertaining to specific health concerns or you think you may be suffering from a medical condition, you should consult a medical professional immediately.

You should also consult a medical professional before making any changes to your normal lifestyle habits.

ISBN: 978-1-7399806-1-0

INTRODUCTION

Hello and welcome to team hearty.

Good luck on your upcoming heart surgery or congratulations for your recovery from a heart attack or open-heart surgery. I know this is a difficult time, and I hope this puzzle book will help to pass the time, be a distraction and stimulate your cognitive function.

The puzzles in this book are all linked to cardiac recovery information, so you can learn about your heart, condition and rehabilitation while you're being distracted and having fun. You may want to Google as some terms you may not be familiar with. There are crosswords, word searches, cryptograms, a little sudoku, and much more.

You'll also find wellness tips and techniques that take 10 minutes or less to do. They can improve your wellbeing, help you relax, distract you and keep you to heal after surgery or a heart attack. They are easy to implement, so you can include them into your daily routine. Plus, I have included inspirational quotes to raise your spirits and keep your hope high.

I'm based in the UK, so some of the spellings and names are English, but there are also some American spellings and terms too. I hope you don't mind, just think of it as raising the difficulty level!

If you're looking for more information on emotional, practical and mental health after an event, I also recommend my other books that are also available from Amazon. The Beat Goes On (practical and emotional help when living with heart disease) and Beyond the Beat (a guide to post surgery and heart attack emotional and mental resilience).

You can read articles and listen to episodes of my podcast from my website www.myheartandmind.co.uk.

You can also help yourself to my free stuff to download to help you on your journey.

- A Guided Relaxation Audio
  www.myheartandmind.co.uk/AD001

- A How to Get Ready to Quit Smoking Guide
  www.myheartandmind.co.uk/HT005

- A How to Prepare for Heart Surgery Checklist
  www.myheartandmind.co.uk/CL002

- A Cardiac Terminology Cheat Sheet
  www.myheartandmind.co.uk/CS003

I wish you a speedy recovery. Remember to take things at your own pace and don't be afraid to ask for help. You've got this!

You are not alone.

Join my Facebook community and meet others just like you. It's for people who have experience of a cardiac event and are having difficulty managing the emotional side of life. It's a safe and nurturing place for you (and your partner) if you have had heart-related problems. Be part of a friendly group of people sharing their own experiences and supporting each other. www.facebook.com/groups/myheartandmindcommunity

CONTENTS

CROSSWORDS

A crossword is a word puzzle that usually takes the form of a square or a rectangular grid of squares. The game's goal is to fill the white squares with letters, forming words or phrases, by solving clues, which lead to the answers. There are no spaces between separate words or phrases as they have been removed.

To enable the crossword grids to be created I have had to include some general knowledge crossword questions.

> *Deep Breathing*
>
> *It helps reduce stress and anxiety by slowing your heart rate and relaxing your muscles. It helps to calm the mind and reduce stress hormones. Sit or lie down in a comfortable position, inhale deeply through your nose, and exhale slowly through your mouth. Repeat for 3-5 minutes.*

Lifestyle Changes 1

ACROSS

1. Roulette bet (3)

2. Pro at giving first aid (3)

4. What habit should you quit to reduce your risk of a cardiac event? (7)

6. Crate-digger's finds (3)

7. Teetotaller's order (8)

8. Baker's baker (4)

9. Recent visitor to U. S. S. R. (5)

10. What substance can build up in your arteries and increase your risk of heart disease? (11)

14. What activity can help improve cardiovascular health? (8)

15. What treatment may be prescribed to help manage high blood pressure or cholesterol? (10)

16. What medical term refers to high blood pressure? (12)

12. What condition can increase your risk of developing heart disease? (8)

24. What type of therapy can help you recover after a cardiac event or surgery? (8, 7)

25. What factor can contribute to high blood pressure and heart disease? (6)

DOWN

1. What condition can increase your risk of heart disease and stroke? (7)

3. Tough call for a bettor (4,2)

5. Saint ___, mother of the Virgin Mary (4)

8. What nutrient can help reduce inflammation and lower your risk of heart disease? (5-1, 5, 5)

6. I must think about this (3,2,3)

11. Successively (3,2,3)

12. What aspect of your lifestyle can affect your cholesterol levels and blood pressure? (4)

13. What factor can increase your risk of developing heart disease, that you can't control? (6, 7)

17. What substance should be consumed in moderation to reduce your risk of a cardiac event? (7)

18. What vital sign should be monitored regularly to help prevent a cardiac event? (5, 8)

19. What mineral should be consumed in moderation to help reduce blood pressure? (6)

20. Indiana Jones' fear (6)

21. Speller's words of clarification (4)

22. Ireland's longest river (7)

23. Give (4)

26. "Young Frankenstein" costar of Cloris and Madeline (4)

27. Bob Fosse specialty (4,5)

You are never too old to set another goal or to dream a new dream. - C.S. Lewis

Cardiac Medications 1

ACROSS

1. Good spots for Peeping Toms (8)

3. Patriot's grp. (3)

6. Blow one's cool (4)

7. What beta-blocker medication is used to treat high blood pressure and angina? (8)

8. What antiplatelet medication is used to prevent blood clots and stroke? (11)

9. Went on a rampage (3, 4)

10. Early August (4)

11. What medication is used to treat chest pain (angina) and heart failure? (10)

14. University professor, e.g. (8)

19. Dismisses derisively (4, 5)

21. Reason someone might do shots? (8)

22. What diuretic medication is used to treat high blood pressure and heart failure? (14)

24. Takeover specialist (6)

27. What calcium channel blocker medication is used to treat high blood pressure and angina? (9)

17. Words in a used car ad (2, 2)

31. Burned residue (3)

32. 1, for one (6)

33. What beta-blocker medication is used to treat high blood pressure, angina, and migraines? (11)

35. Foremost (3)

36. What statin medication is used to lower cholesterol and reduce the risk of heart attack and stroke? (11)

DOWN

2. Was a benchwarmer (3)

4. Zero, to Cash (4)

5. Allocate (7)

7. What is the medication called Lisinopril? (3, 9)

12. What medication is used to treat high blood pressure, angina, and heart failure? (10)

13. "The Mask of ___" (5)

15. Longtime pop group with mostly self-named albums (7)

16. Very exciting contest (8)

17. Earl in the Baseball Hall of Fame (7)

18. What "Jumping Jack Flash" is (1, 3)

20. What medication is used to treat chest pain quickly? (5-8)

23. Kitchen staple (7)

25. What ACE inhibitor medication is used to treat high blood pressure and heart failure? (9)

26. What antiarrhythmic medication is used to treat atrial and ventricular arrhythmias? (9)

28. 'Pb' element (4)

29. What beta-blocker is used to treat high blood pressure? (10)

30. Extremes at Wimbledon (4, 5)

34. What calcium channel blocker medication is used to treat high blood pressure, angina, and arrhythmias? (9)

Psychological Therapies

ACROSS

1. Addressing long-standing patterns of maladaptive thoughts? (6, 7, 9)

3. Creating a supportive and non-judgmental therapeutic environment? (6, 7)

6. Magazine VIPs (7)

7. Get into (3)

9. Using childlike activities to communicate and resolve psychological issues? (4)

10. La Brea goop (3)

12. Shore-dinner item (4)

13. Emphasizes the whole and the here-and-now experience? (7)

15. Cultivating present-moment awareness for stress relief? (11)

16. Suit, so to speak (9)

17. Exploring unconscious patterns and early life experiences? (13)

19. Acting out internal conflicts and exploring alternative behaviours? (11)

21. Kids always lose them (4, 5)

24. Whimsical alternative to "voila!" (3)

25. Like Polish jokes and "woman driver" comments (2, 2)

29. Arkin of "Glengarry Glen Ross" (4)

30. Challenging irrational beliefs for emotional well-being? (8, 7, 9)

33. Using horses to facilitate emotional growth and healing? (6, 8)

35. Using creative expression for psychological exploration and healing? (3, 7)

36. Examining the meaning and purpose of life? (11)

37. Processing traumatic experiences through eye movements? (4)

DOWN

2. Balancing acceptance and change in behaviour? (11, 9)

4. Working with and processing emotions for therapeutic change? (7, 7)

5. Restructuring personal stories for healing and growth? (9)

8. Tar's affirmatives (4)

11. Exploring the connection between language, thoughts, and behaviour? (5-10, 11)

14. Changing thoughts and behaviours for a healthier mind? (9, 11)

18. Understanding individuals within the context of household dynamics? (6, 7)

20. Using magnetic fields to stimulate brain regions? (11, 8, 11)

22. Using trance to access and modify the subconscious? (12)

23. Analysis of the psyche may uncover hidden meanings? (14)

1. Focusing on solutions rather than dwelling on problems? (8, 7, 5)

26. Sign of good reception? (4, 4)

27. Identifying and changing deeply ingrained patterns of thinking? (6)

28. Accepting difficult thoughts and emotions while taking action? (10, 3, 10)

31. Using physiological feedback to gain control over bodily processes? (11)

32. Sheltered, as stock (7)

34. Incorporating multiple therapeutic approaches for holistic treatment? (11)

Cardiac Terminology 1

ACROSS

1. What medical device is used to record the heart's activity over a period of 24-48 hours? (6, 7)

3. Kind of ruler (8)

4. Sailor's behind? (6)

5. What is the medical term for the build-up of plaque in the arteries? (15)

6. South American capital (5)

7. What medical test uses sound waves to create images of the heart? (14)

13. Broke (8)

14. What medical condition involves abnormal heart sounds, which can be caused by a variety of factors? (5, 6)

15. First-founded state capital (5,2)

18. What heart condition causes an irregular heartbeat and can increase the risk of stroke? (6, 12)

20. G-man (5)

27. Like jogging or rowing (7)

29. Aesthete's concern (4)

30. National songs (7)

31. Stand buy (8)

32. Spice (9)

34. Either of two cities that share a state border (9)

35. Hip-hop's Salt-_-_ (1,4)

37. What general term describes a range of conditions that affect the heart? (5, 7)

DOWN

2. Bygone comic strip (8)

5. Pathogen combatant (4,5)

8. "I don't ___ want to think about it!" (4)

9. Essential oils (6)

10. Composer of "The Seasons" (5)

1. What event occurs when blood flow to the heart is blocked, causing damage to the heart muscle? (5, 6)

11. What device is used to deliver an electric shock to the heart to restore normal heart rhythm? (13)

12. What waxy substance can build up in the arteries and increase the risk of heart disease? (11)

16. Get some shuteye (4)

17. "The Da Vinci Code" villain (5)

19. What is the medical procedure used to open blocked or narrowed arteries? (11)

21. Bonnie of "Die Hard" (7)

22. Eat like a mouse (4)

23. Precipitated by (5)

24. What device is implanted under the skin to help regulate the heart's rhythm? (9)

25. Allowing for contingencies (4, 5)

26. What is the condition when the arteries that supply blood to the heart become narrow or blocked? (8, 6, 7)

14. What condition occurs when the force of blood against the walls of the arteries is too high? (4, 5, 8)

28. Goes here and there (4)

33. Vague number (7)

32. What heart condition occurs when the heart can't pump enough blood to meet the body's needs? (10, 5, 7)

36. What medical procedure involves threading a catheter through a blood vessel to the heart to diagnose or treat heart conditions? (7, 15)

Hospital Related

ACROSS

1. TV tavern keeper (3)

3. Cricket ___ (3)

4. A hospital unit that provides specialised care for critically ill patients? (9, 4, 4)

7. A doctor who performs surgery? (7)

9. A tube inserted into the body for the purpose of draining fluids or administering medications? (8)

10. Clothing worn by hospital staff during surgeries and procedures? (6)

13. Sudden shock of electricity (4)

14. Unimportant matter (3,5)

17. Used for transporting patients in a hospital? (6)

18. Lesser ___ (bearcat) (5)

19. The branch of medicine that focuses on the heart and circulatory system? (10)

22. A test that uses X-rays and computer technology to create detailed pictures of the body? (2, 4)

25. A test that records the electrical activity of the heart? (3)

26. A hospital department that provides immediate medical care for serious illnesses and injuries? (9, 4)

31. Condition of TV's Monk, for short (3)

32. A professional who helps patients regain their ability to perform daily activities? (12, 9)

34. Peter the Great's title (4)

36. A patient who is admitted to the hospital for treatment? (9)

38. A room in a hospital for patients? (4)

39. A person who receives medical treatment? (7)

40. An imaging test that uses radiation to create pictures of the body? (1-3)

DOWN

2. Gives off, as an odour (5)

5. "Born Free" author Joy (7)

6. The release of a patient from the hospital after treatment? (9)

8. Used to close wounds? (7)

10. An instrument used for listening to heart and lung sounds? (11)

11. Medication used to prevent pain during surgery? (11)

12. An imaging test that uses a magnetic field and radio waves to create pictures of the body? (3)

15. The administration of fluids or medications through an IV? (8)

16. Anne and Agathe e.g. (4)

3. A device used to measure a patient's blood pressure? (5, 8, 4)

20. "Deuce Coupe" choreographer Twyla (5)

21. Sudden energetic spurt (5)

23. Measurements of a patient's temperature, pulse, respiration, and blood pressure? (5, 5)

24. A patient who receives treatment without being admitted to the hospital? (10)

27. Bite-sized cookie (4,4)

28. A doctor who specialises in caring for hospitalised patients? (11)

29. Barracks bugaboo (3)

30. A healthcare professional who provides care to patients? (5)

33. The branch of medicine that uses imaging techniques to diagnose and treat diseases? (9)

35. A vehicle used for transporting patients to the hospital? (9)

37. A room in a hospital where surgeries are performed? (9, 4)

41. A doctor who specialises in administering anaesthesia? (17)

42. The department in a hospital that dispenses medications? (8)

Exercise & Activity

ACROSS

1. Sen. Booker of New Jersey (4)

4. Piece of esoterica (7)

7. Word that's often confused with "imply" (5)

9. What exercise involves lowering one's body by bending at the knees and hips? (9)

13. Game co. that originated Dungeons Dragons (3)

14. Common ID (7)

15. What activity involves walking in nature on a trail or in the wilderness? (6)

17. Rejected (4, 2)

19. What martial art involves slow, controlled movements and deep breathing? (3, 3)

20. Tick off (5)

21. What activity involves moving one's body to music in a rhythmic way? (7)

24. What activity involves riding a bicycle for exercise or transportation? (7)

28. Relaxing getaway spot (3)

29. 90 percent, say (4)

31. Whole (7)

34. Prize in horse racing (5)

36. What activity involves propelling a boat through water using oars? (6)

37. Garbage-hauling boat (4)

DOWN

2. It may prey on a ray (4)

3. What practice involves physical postures, breathing techniques, and meditation or relaxation? (4)

5. Area with pews (4)

6. What activity involves propelling oneself off the ground using one's legs? (7)

8. What sport involves two or four players hitting a ball over a net with rackets? (6)

10. What activity involves moving through water using one's arms and legs? (8)

11. Hawaii's predecessor as a state (6)

12. What activity involves moving rapidly on foot, typically on a track or road? (7)

16. What exercise system involves controlled movements to strengthen the core and improve flexibility? (7)

18. What activity involves lifting heavy weights to build strength and muscle mass? (13)

22. Basketball player Archibald (4)

23. What sport involves two teams trying to score points by shooting a ball into a basket? (10)

20. What activity involves lengthening one's muscles to improve flexibility and prevent injury? (9)

25. What sport involves two teams trying to keep a ball in the air and over a net? (10)

26. Vesicles (5)

27. What activity involves gliding on snow using skis attached to one's feet? (6)

30. Signifies (8)

32. What activity involves moving at a moderate pace on foot? (7)

33. What activity involves jumping over a rope that is swung by oneself or others? (4, 4)

35. What sport involves two teams trying to score goals by kicking a ball into the opposing team's net? (6)

1
2
3
4
5
6
7
8
9
10
11
12
13
14
15
16
17
18
19
20
21
22
23
24
25
26
27
28
29
30
31
32
33
34
35
36
37

Parts of the Heart 1

ACROSS

1. What artery branches into the left anterior descending artery and the circumflex artery? (4, 8, 6)

2. What blood vessel supplies oxygen and nutrients to the heart muscle itself? (8, 6)

5. Temple gateway in Japan (5)

6. "Physician, heal ___" (7)

7. German communications centre in W.W. II (2,2)

8. What artery branches off from the aorta and supplies blood to the right arm and head? (15, 6)

9. What is the outer layer of the heart wall called? (10)

12. Was too fond (5)

13. Bus. card info, perhaps (3)

15. Someone from north of the border? (4)

16. "What Kind of Fool ___" (2,1)

21. Which chamber of the heart pumps oxygenated blood to the rest of the body? (4, 9)

26. What is the electrical relay station that allows the atria to fully contract before the ventricles contract called? (16, 4)

28. Freud's "The __ and the Id" (3)

23. What is the inner lining of the heart called? (11)

31. Memorable swimsuit model Cheryl (5)

34. Underlying cause (4)

DOWN

1. What is the artery that supplies blood to the left ventricle, also known as the "widowmaker"? (4, 8, 10, 6)

3. What are the tough, fibrous cords that connect the papillary muscles to the heart valves? (7, 9)

4. Cheers at a corrida (4)

10. What is the large vein on the back of the heart that collects blood from the coronary circulation? (8, 5)

11. Celebrate, as a holiday (7)

14. What separates the left ventricle from the aorta? (6, 5)

17. Ingredient in a gin-based liqueur (4)

18. Tenor Schipa (4)

19. Which large vein carries deoxygenated blood from the lower body to the heart? (8, 4, 4)

20. What is the wall that separates the left and right ventricles called? (16, 6)

22. Salon specialties (4)

23. Decorative sewing bag (4)

24. What is the largest artery in the body? (5)

25. Heated conflict (3,2)

27. Dime's worth (3,5)

29. Flours (6)

30. Gun in many an action flick (3)

32. Greg's sitcom partner (6)

33. Rolls, so to speak (4)

21. Which chamber of the heart receives oxygenated blood from the lungs? (4, 6)

Cardiac Terminology 2

ACROSS

1. Not anti (4)

3. Appliance with a lint trap (5)

4. What condition involves an irregular heartbeat? (10)

5. What event occurs when the heart suddenly stops beating? (7, 6)

8. What condition involves a feeling of skipped or extra heartbeats? (5, 12)

13. Cloak like garment (6)

16. Minuet, e.g. (5)

18. Songbird's sound (5)

19. What condition involves inflammation of the inner lining of the heart? (12)

23. Just manage (3,2)

24. What condition involves an enlarged or thickened heart muscle? (14)

26. What medical procedure involves replacing a heart flap? (5, 11)

27. Washington WNBA team (7)

30. What condition can damage the heart valves and is caused by untreated strep throat? (9, 5)

31. Quarterback target (3)

34. Really tickle (5)

35. What condition involves inflammation of the heart muscle? (11)

37. Astute (4)

DOWN

2. What condition involves a heart rate that is too fast? (11)

6. What event occurs when blood flow to the brain is blocked, causing damage to brain cells? (6)

7. Low-tech clicker (8)

9. Thing that might be brought up in a street fight (4)

10. What condition involves inflammation of the sac that surrounds the heart? (12)

11. Adjusts, as a trip counter (6)

12. Remains. (5)

14. Intent on (4)

15. Consecrates (7)

17. What condition involves irregular and rapid heartbeats that can be life-threatening? (11, 12)

20. Follow-up to the "Thriller" album (3)

21. Sheik land (6)

22. What event occurs when a blood clot travels to the lungs and blocks blood flow? (9, 8)

25. What test involves monitoring the heart's activity during exercise or given drugs? (6, 4)

28. Business brass (4)

29. What event is commonly known as a "mini-stroke" ? (9, 8, 6)

32. Emo, for example (5)

33. Kind of memory (8)

36. "Casablanca" co-star (5)

38. Blueprint with four bases (3)

1
2
10
7
6
5
38
21
15
17
23
16
9
14
8
12
3
4
11
20
13
29
18
25
24
31
22
33
34
36
19
30
35
27
32
28
26
37

Cardiology Team

ACROSS

1. Edward, to buddies (3)

3. Who helps patients recover from heart surgeries and procedures? (7, 14, 10)

6. Problem for prima Donnas (4)

8. Cheerful and delighted (4)

9. Which surgeon performs surgeries on the heart, lungs, and chest? (14)

12. Totals (4,2,2)

13. Substantiate (6)

15. Which cardiologist performs procedures to diagnose and treat heart conditions? (14)

16. Who keeps you quiet during heart surgeries and procedures? (7, 18)

17. Presses clothes (5)

20. Temporary suspension of breathing (5)

21. Fork over formally (5)

23. Which medical professional specialises in treating heart conditions? (12)

29. Navigator's creator (8)

30. Darts shooter (5)

32. What scripts are written for (4)

35. Ammo storehouses (8)

36. Scheldt feeder (3)

38. Drawing tool for engineers (3,6)

39. What type of nurse specialises in caring for patients with heart conditions? (7, 5)

40. Japanese theatre (3)

DOWN

2. Goes by (7)

4. Make an edging. (3)

5. Who uses ultrasound to create images of the heart for diagnosis and monitoring? (17)

7. Glazed (3)

10. Cow with a drawn-out look (6, 4)

11. Who conducts studies related to heart and blood vessel disorders? (13, 10)

14. Snoopy's red opponent (5)

18. "Sesame Street" character (4)

19. Who performs and interprets tests that measure electrical activity in the heart? (17, 10)

22. Sound stages (4)

24. Which surgeon specialises in treating blood vessel disorders? (8)

25. Who operates the heart-lung machine during open-heart surgeries? (12)

26. Restaurant offering (4)

27. Who assists in diagnosing and treating heart and blood vessel conditions? (13, 12)

28. Which cardiologist specialises in treating heart rhythm disorders? (18)

31. Who assists with diagnostic and interventional procedures for heart conditions? (15, 3, 5)

33. Who performs and interprets tests that assess heart structure and function? (7, 10)

34. Who manages and coordinates clinical trials related to cardiology? (8, 8, 11)

37. Electrified particles (4)

41. Who specialises in prescribing and managing medications for heart conditions? (7, 10)

42. Who performs echocardiograms to assess heart function? (7, 11)

Investigations & Tests 1

ACROSS

1. Props for Astaire (5)

4. Discard, animal style (4)

6. 1/6 of a fluid ounce (3)

7. What uses a magnetic field and radio waves to create images of the heart? (3)

9. What device records the heart's activity over a period of time? (6, 7)

11. F.B.I. machine (8)

12. Popular "The Price Is Right" prize (3)

14. What uses sound waves to create images of the heart? (14)

19. Zen enlightenment (6)

18. What measures the electrical activity of the heart? (3)

20. Unglamorous assignment (5,3)

22. Church choral works (6)

24. Bluish-grey in colour (5)

27. Tablet with E Ink (4)

28. One in an audience (8)

31. Tracy Morgan book "I ___ New Black" (2,3)

32. Go quickly (3)

33. Shows disapproval of (4)

DOWN

2. Asics competitor (4)

3. Bad marks? (7)

5. 1400 hours (3,2)

8. Coins in India (6)

10. Lunch box dessert item (4)

13. Agenda thing (4)

15. What uses a special probe inserted through the mouth and is also known as TEE? (16, 14)

16. Clodhopper (6)

17. What uses X-rays to visualize the blood vessels in the heart? (8, 9)

18. Cause to be resentful (8)

21. What measures how the heart responds to physical activity? (8, 6, 4)

23. Flight named for its effect on fliers (3,3)

12. What uses X-rays to create detailed images of the heart? (2, 4)

25. Much-loved star (4)

26. What involves injecting a radioactive tracer to evaluate blood flow to the heart? (10, 9, 7)

29. What involves the insertion of a thin tube into the heart to measure blood flow and pressure? (7, 15)

30. Government group that approves new medications (4)

When you come out of the storm, you won't be the same person who walked in. That's what this storm's all about.

- Haruki Murakami

Lifestyle Changes 2

ACROSS

1. What medication may be recommended to help reduce the risk of blood clots? (7)

4. Visitor to Venus (7)

5. Three-term Big Apple mayor (2,4)

6. "Calling all cars" message (3)

8. Eat crow, formally (7)

9. What factor can contribute to obesity and increase your risk of heart disease? (10)

11. Central positions (6)

17. What food should be consumed in moderation to help reduce the risk of heart disease? (3, 4)

18. Question of technique (3)

20. Aid offer (3.2)

22. Secretive couple (7)

23. Real beauty (3)

24. What goal may be recommended for overweight or obese individuals to help improve cardiovascular health? (6, 4)

25. What program can help you improve your cardiovascular health after a cardiac event or surgery? (7, 14)

26. What type of grains are rich in fibre and can help reduce cholesterol levels? (5, 6)

27. What stimulant should be consumed in moderation to help reduce the risk of high blood pressure? (8)

29. Some sedimentary rocks (6)

30. What condition can increase your risk of high blood pressure and heart disease? (5, 6)

DOWN

2. What type of fat should be consumed in moderation to help reduce the risk of heart disease? (9, 4)

3. Georgia Tech's Sam ___ School of International Affairs (4)

7. A few hours of relaxing, say (2,4)

8. Genetic substance, for short (3)

10. What calculation is used to assess whether someone is underweight, normal weight, overweight, or obese? (4, 4, 5)

12. What type of fat should be avoided to help reduce your risk of heart disease? (5, 4)

13. What mineral is important but should be consumed in moderation to help reduce the risk of heart disease? (7)

14. Locales for rest stops (4,5)

15. Home to domesticated insects (4)

16. What food group should be consumed in abundance to help improve cardiovascular health? (6, 3, 10)

19. Gridiron ritual (4)

21. What type of diet has been shown to help improve cardiovascular health? (13, 4)

28. What term refers to any movement that increases energy expenditure? (8, 8)

Heart Healthy Food

ACROSS

1. Satellite inhabited continuously since 2000 (3)

3. What breakfast food is high in fibre and can help lower cholesterol? (7)

6. City in a Cole Porter tune (5)

9. Capone, Franken, and Pacino (3)

10. What cooking oil is rich in monounsaturated fats? (5, 3)

14. Indy 500 letters (3)

5. What type of fish is a good source of omega-3 fatty acids and vitamin D? (4)

16. What beverage contains antioxidants that can help protect the heart and lower blood pressure? (5, 3)

17. City on New Providence (6)

21. Flamenco dancer's clicker (8)

23. Where the Ussuri flows (4)

24. Which leafy green is a good source of potassium and magnesium? (7)

26. Polar expedition vehicles (7)

27. What root vegetable is high in fibre and contains vitamins A and C? (5, 8)

34. What whole grain is a good source of fibre and contains selenium, which can help protect the heart? (5, 4)

35. What nut is a good source of heart-healthy fats? (7)

37. Which fruit is rich in antioxidants that help lower blood pressure? (11)

DOWN

2. Politician Harold (7)

4. Alter to fit. (5)

5. What fruit contains lycopene, which can help reduce the risk of heart disease? (8)

7. What fruit is high in vitamin C and contains flavonoids that can help lower blood pressure? (7)

8. Acts hangdog (5)

11. "___ This, Not That!" (diet book) (3)

12. What grain is high in protein and contains heart-healthy unsaturated fats? (6)

13. Worn things (4)

15. What legume is a good source of fibre and contains folate and magnesium? (9)

18. What fruit contains pectin, a type of fibre that can help lower cholesterol? (6)

19. What heart-healthy food is high in monounsaturated fat? (7)

20. What alcoholic beverage contains resveratrol, which can help improve heart health? (3, 4)

22. Inflicts corporal punishment on (6)

25. Turns a certain way (7)

28. Shin bone (5)

29. What sweet treat contains flavonoids that can help reduce blood pressure? (4, 9)

30. Insomniac's wish (5)

31. What dairy product is high in calcium and contains probiotics that can help improve gut health? (6)

32. What type of fish is high in omega-3 fatty acids? (6)

33. Teddy ___ (Nabisco product) (7)

34. What vegetable is high in fibre and contains antioxidants that can help protect the heart? (8)

36. New money in '99 (4)

Parts of the Heart 2

ACROSS

1. What chamber of the heart receives deoxygenated blood from the body? (5, 6)

3. Baldwin's father on "30 Rock" (4)

4. Expert, so to speak (5)

5. Animated greetings (6)

7. The bride in Wagner's "Bridal Chorus" (4)

9. Manual (5)

11. "The Tonight Show" host (4)

12. Which vessel carries oxygenated blood from the lungs to the heart? (9, 4)

14. Love too much (4)

16. In close relation. (8)

19. Seek damages (3)

20. Turnip (8)

21. What is the middle, muscular layer of the heart wall called? (10)

23. Work with a number, often (4)

24. Woolly beast (5)

26. Antipoverty agcy. created by LBJ (hidden in SHOE ORGANISER) (3)

17. What is the sac that surrounds and protects the heart called? (11)

27. P. Drake's portrayer in a big lie (7)

18. What muscular wall divides the left and right sides of the heart? (6)

29. What valve separates the right ventricle from the pulmonary artery? (9, 5)

30. Story boards? (6)

DOWN

2. What valve separates the right atrium from the right ventricle? (9, 5)

6. What is the muscular band in the right ventricle that helps coordinate contractions? (9, 4)

8. Overly harsh (9)

10. What valve controls the flow of blood between the left atrium and left ventricle? (7, 5)

7. Youngster's sch. (4)

13. What artery supplies blood to the right atrium? (5, 8)

15. Ship featured in a 1997 megafilm (7)

17. Which artery carries deoxygenated blood from the heart to the lungs? (9, 6)

18. Resort with mineral springs (3)

1. Which chamber of the heart pumps deoxygenated blood to the lungs? (5, 9)

19. They're sometimes running (6)

22. What is the natural pacemaker of the heart? (10, 4)

25. Mariner's org. (4)

28. What muscle contracts to prevent the backflow of blood through the mitral and tricuspid valves? (9, 6)

31. Which large vein carries deoxygenated blood from the upper body to the heart? (8, 4, 4)

Every day is a new beginning. Take a deep breath, smile and start again. - Unknown

Cardiac Medications 2

ACROSS

1. One that heads up the staff (4)

2. Marcos with a shoe collection (6)

3. "River" blue (4)

5. What type helps to widen blood vessels and improve blood flow to the heart? (12)

7. Org. promoting intelligence (3)

8. What is used to treat chronic angina? (10)

10. What is used to prevent blood clots and reduce the risk of stroke? (8)

14. What type helps to remove excess fluid from the body and reduce blood pressure? (9)

16. What is used to lower cholesterol levels and reduce the risk of heart attack and stroke? (12)

17. Drive (5)

22. What is used to prevent blood clots? (8)

24. Start of a show-off kid's cry (4,2)

26. What is used to reduce the risk of blood clots and heart attack? (8)

27. What type is used to lower cholesterol levels and reduce the risk of heart attack? (7)

29. Game with a body board (9)

30. What is used to blood clots building up in newly fitted stents? (10)

31. Reach capacity, slangily, with "out" (3)

32. What is used to prevent blood clots and DVTs? (7)

33. Fat, e.g. (5)

35. Browser entry, briefly (3)

DOWN

1. What type helps to relax blood vessels and lower blood pressure? (7,7,8)

4. What is used to control arrhythmias? (10)

6. What is used to relieve chest pain (angina) caused by reduced blood flow to the heart? (5-9)

9. What is used to lower blood pressure and improve blood flow to the heart? (8)

11. What type helps to widen blood vessels and reduce blood pressure? (3, 10)

12. Pay the kitty (4)

13. What is used to treat high blood pressure and reduce fluid build-up in the body? (10)

15. Jacobin revolutionary who was stabbed in a bathtub (5)

18. What is used to treat high blood pressure and chest pain (angina)? (10)

19. Rodents (5)

20. What type slows the heart rate and reduces blood pressure? (4-8)

21. "That's a great price!" (5,4)

23. Quadrant's relatives (8)

25. Marble type (5)

28. What is used to prevent chest pain (angina) caused by reduced blood flow to the heart? (10,11)

34. What is used to control irregular heartbeats? (7)

1
21
20
2
4
27
13
17
6
18
33
5
3
24
7
11
14
28
19
15
10
12
35
8
9
23
31
16
22
25
29
26
34
32
30

Investigations & Tests 2

ACROSS

1. They have headboards and footboards (4)
4. Black-throated ___ (Asian bird) (3)
6. "If God had wanted us to vote, he would have given us candidates" comic (4)
7. Build on, with "to" (3)
8. Prepares for use, as software (8)
10. Intend, in Scotland (5)
12. What uses CT imaging to visualize the blood vessels in the heart? (7, 2, 11)
13. What uses an ultrasound probe inserted into the blood vessels to create images of the heart? (12, 10)
14. Place to play cards (6)
19. The entirety (3)
20. Aetna's business (3)
21. 1,051, in old Rome (3)
22. What combines an echocardiogram with an exercise? (6, 13)
23. Shoe-factory worker (5)
24. Place to store wood (4)
25. Organisation for mums, dads, and pedagogues (3)
26. What measures the electrical activity of the heart to identify and treat arrhythmias? (3)
27. ___ server (site from which to download) (3)
28. Battle of Britain heroes (3)
29. Rock or horse follower (5)
30. What measures the pressure and blood flow in the coronary arteries to evaluate blockages? (10, 4, 7)

DOWN

2. Copious unwanted advice (6)
3. Faineance (5)
5. Astringent (6)
8. Happening (8)
9. What uses a radioactive tracer to create images of the heart? (12, 7)
11. What is used to evaluate the cause of fainting episodes? (4, 5, 4)
15. What uses CT imaging to check for calcium deposits in the heart? (5, 4)
16. Dept. once headed by Gen. Hershey (3)
17. Crusoe's longtime home (4)
18. What uses MRI to visualize the blood vessels in the heart? (7, 8, 9, 11)
14. Johnny Appleseed's real name (7)
29. Canyon colour (5)
31. River to the Volga near Gorky (3)
32. What is used to diagnose arrhythmias? (6-8, 17)

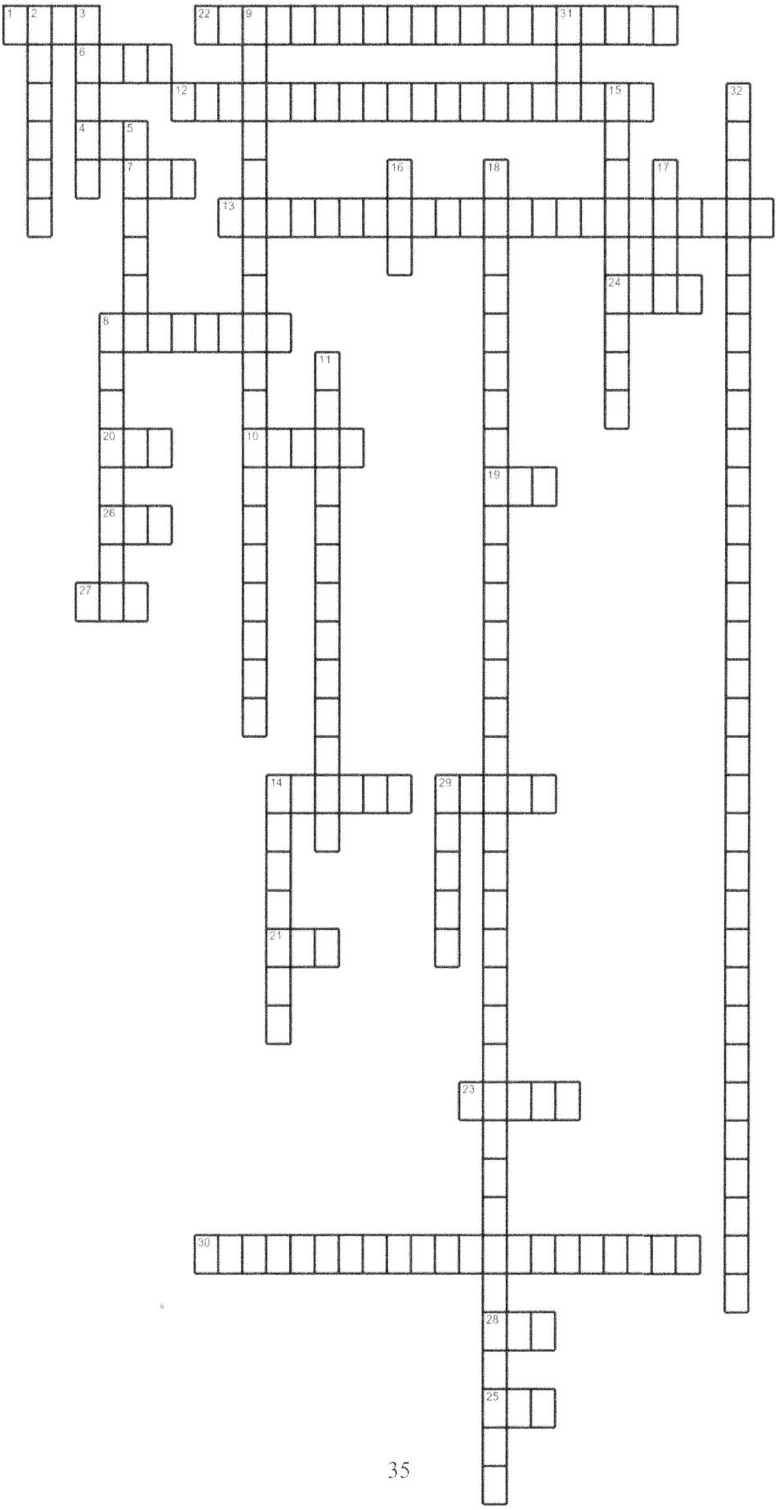
1
2
3
4
5
6
7
8
9
10
11
12
13
14
15
16
17
18
19
20
21
22
23
24
25
26
27
28
29
30
31
32

CRYPTOGRAMS

A cryptogram is a type of puzzle that consists of a short piece of encrypted text.

Cryptograms based on ciphers can often be solved by frequency analysis and by recognising letter patterns in words, such as one letter words, which, in English, can only be "i" or "a" (and sometimes "o").

To solve the puzzle, one must recover the original lettering. I have included some hints at the end of this section if required.

> Laugh Therapy
>
> Laughter helps reduce stress and anxiety by releasing endorphins and boosting your mood. Search for a funny video on YouTube. TikTok. or Instagram. Watch it for 10 minutes and allow yourself to laugh out loud. Laughter is contagious. so get a friend to laugh with you.

HEARTIE PHRASE CRYPTOGRAMS

01.

F	D	T	U	K		Z	T	K	K	D	U	N

--

02.

V	L	S	S	L	X		O	L	W	T		E	G	Q	T	Y

--

03.

I	G	J		V	L	K		R	K	I	V		S	X	K	E

X	G

--

04.

M	Q	Q	F		X	B	Y	H		B	I	W		O	B	G	Q

Z	Q	B	E	N

--

05.

F	U	M	K		W	X	D	L		B	K	U	T	F	B

F	X		B	K	U	L	F

--

HEARTIE PHRASE CRYPTOGRAMS

06.

Q	O	C	D		D	O	I		P	K	D		X	O	C	D	N

I	Z	M	O	C	M	O

--

07.

G	C	K	’	Y		O	J	S	C		J		O	C	J	M	K

K	Q		O	C	J	M	K

--

08.

F	U	D	S		P	K	V	Q		J	S	R	Q	L		R

J	S	R	X		Z	L	R	Q	L

--

09.

I	W	V		C	I	G	G	,		N	Q	J	I

N	Q	U	I	,		G	D	J	I		G	Q	L	X

--

Your present circumstances don't determine where you can go; they merely determine where you start. - Nido Qubein

HEARTIE PHRASE CRYPTOGRAMS

10.

OXR RD RMX MXPVR

DE RMX QPRRXV

--

11.

VU XUKJ HGJQ, ZGJB

WUJ XUKJ PBGJQ

--

12.

MNKD ZCH QKWCZ,

ZYHTZ GNSY CHTYZ

YKWCZ

--

Progressive Muscle Relaxation

It helps reduce tension and promote relaxation by increasing body awareness. Sit or lie down in a comfortably. Starting with your feet, tense the muscles and hold for a few seconds, then release. Work your way up your body to the top of your head, tensing and relaxing each muscle group. Do this for about 5 minutes.

HEARTIE PHRASE CRYPTOGRAMS

13.

E		V	T	E	A	J	V	Z

V	T	E	K	J	N	T	E	J		R	Y		E

Q	G	X	H	T	K	P	D	A		J	K	T	E	J

--

14.

K	S		Y	N	N	W	D		D	F		D	G	N	N	S

S	F		V	O	T	N		O		V	N	O	W	S	V	B

V	N	O	Q	S		I	N	O	S

--

15.

C	M	K	J	M		R	K	W	Y		O	K	U

N	X	M	Y		K		P	J	K	M	R	Z	E	F

K	V	O		Y	R	K	F	M	Y	U		Y	R	K	J	M

--

HEARTIE PHRASE CRYPTOGRAMS - HINTS

01.	K => T, T => A, U => R	**09.**	Q => O, D => I, I => E
02.	O => Y, L => O, X => W	**10.**	R => T, X => E, M => H
03.	V => T, X => O, E => S	**11.**	B => E, H => P, G => A
04.	Q => E, X => C, Z => H	**12.**	N => O, K => I, Z => T
05.	K => E, L => R, B => H	**13.**	E => A, D => U, H => D
06.	D => R, O => E, P => F	**14.**	D => S, S => T, I => B
07.	J => A, Y => S, C => E	**15.**	J => R, N => W, F => L
08.	D => V, V => U, S => E		

I can't change the direction of the wind, but I can adjust my sails to always reach my destination. - Jimmy Dean

SUDOKU

Sudoku is a 9x9 grid puzzle game.

The objective is to fill the 9×9 grid with digits so that each column, each row, and each of the nine 3×3 sub grids that compose the grid (also called "boxes", "blocks", or "regions") contain all of the digits from 1 to 9.

You are provided a partially completed puzzle to complete, with a single solution. There are 4 difficulty levels Easy, Intermediate, Hard and Insane.

> Talk to a friend
>
> Talking to a friend can help reduce stress and improve mood. It can help you feel connected and supported. Don't be shy, reach out not only will it help you feel great but your friend will too. Call or text a friend and chat for 10 minutes.

GRID - 1

Easy

	1	8	3	9	4		5	
	6	7	1		5			
			6	2		8	9	1
8	5	6			1	4	2	9
	2			4	8	1	6	3
1		3	9		2	5	7	8
		1		7			3	4
6	7		2		3		8	5
	8						1	6

GRID - 2

Easy

	7	2	6	9	5	8	1	
		9			1			
			8	7		6		2
	5	4			8	2	3	9
9	3			2		1	4	8
1	2	8	4		9	7		5
		5		8				7
6	9	3	7		2		8	1
2	8			1		3	5	6

GRID - 3

Easy

8	2	3				1	6	
	7	5		6		4	9	8
4	9	6	1		8	2	7	3
	6	8		1	3			4
7	1	9		4	5		8	2
3						6	1	
	3	1	2	8	6	5	4	
		7	4	3	1			
				7			3	1

GRID - 4

Easy

8	1		4		7	5		
			9	8		7	6	2
9	7		3	5		8	1	
5			6		9			1
2		8	7	1	3		4	
			8	4		2		6
7	8	4	2	3	6	1	5	
1	3	9	5	7	4			8
			1		8	4	3	

GRID - 5

Easy

2		8		1			7	6
4		6	9	3		5	8	
5	1		6	7		4		3
	6		1			8	4	5
1		2	7		4	3	6	
			8		6			2
	9	3				1		4
8	4	1	5	6	9	2		
	2		3	4	1	6	9	

GRID - 6

Easy

1	2		7	4	6	9		3
9					5		6	7
	5	6	3		9	4	8	
2	4		9	5	8	1		6
			2	3	7	5		4
	9	3	4			8		
3		5		8	4	7		9
				9	3			8
6	8	9	1		2	3		5

GRID - 7

Easy

4	8		7		3	6		
7	5		9	2		4	8	3
	3				8	7		2
8	9		5	7	6			4
	4					8	3	7
2	1	7		8	4		6	9
1	2		4	3			7	6
5		9				3		
	6	4		9	7	2	1	5

GRID - 8

Easy

2		7	6		4	1	8	9
	9		1	7			3	6
	6	1	3		9	2		7
		5			6	8	4	2
	7	2	4				9	3
3	4				8		1	
	5			4			2	1
	8	9	2	6	3		7	4
7			5	9	1		6	8

GRID - 5

Intermediate

7	6	3		9			4	2
8		2		7	6	5		
		4		8	2			7
	2	6	8		7			4
	8			3				6
	4		6	5			7	
4		8		2	5	3		9
	3	5				7	2	1
2	7	9	1	6	3	4		

GRID - 6

Intermediate

		4				7	3	
2		8				5	9	6
9	7	3		6				4
4		7		1	3	2	6	
		5	6	8	9			
	9	6	4	7	2	1	5	8
8	3		9	2		4		5
			8	3	4	6	2	
		2		5	1	9	8	

Believe you can and you're halfway there.
- Theodore Roosevelt

GRID - 7

Intermediate

9	3	1		4				8
2	4		1	7	5	9		6
6			3			1	4	2
	8	3	9	2			5	
		6		8	1		9	
4			5	3				1
			4		7		8	
				5			6	4
	5		2	6	3	7		9

GRID - 8

Intermediate

				4	2		5	
2	1	5	8	3			9	4
8		7	1		9			2
			5	6	4			9
	5	4		2		1	6	
9		2	3	1	7		8	5
	7		4	8				6
1	2	8			3			
4	3	6	2	7	5			8

GRID - 1

Hard

	8		7			3	2	5
5		2	3	6		4	1	
	4	3	5					
7	1				2	6	5	
2			8	5			9	
	9	5				2		3
	5				1	9	4	2
		1	4	9		5		7
				7	5		3	8

GRID - 2

Hard

	8	4	5	7	9			
	6				1	9	5	7
9			3			1	8	
				4	7	8		3
3		9					4	2
		6					1	
7		8	1				3	5
6	2			5				
		5	6	9	8	2	7	1

GRID - 3

Hard

			2	7			1	
6	1	7	9	5		8		
2	8	9					3	7
8			5	9	1		4	
5		1		4		7		
4	2	3	6					
			7	2	5	4		3
		2						8
				1	9	2		5

GRID - 4

Hard

4				8		9		3
			4				6	1
	1	3	6	5		2	4	
9			3		2	5		6
	5					4	3	2
3			1	6		8		
	4		2	3			9	
	3						8	
		7	9	1		3	2	5

GRID - 5

Hard

7	1					8		
	4			9	5	6		
6	3			1		7	4	9
1			9		8	4		5
	8		1			9	3	
5								8
9	6	1		3				4
	5	4				3	7	
3		7		8	1			6

GRID - 6

Hard

		5	4			2		8
	9		5		7	4	3	1
7		4				5		
			2				5	3
2	7	1						
	8	3		6		7		9
		2		4		8		
6	1	7		8			4	
9	4	8	7	5			6	2

GRID - 7

Hard

			5				3	
	4	5	6	2	3	1		7
	2		1	8	7			
	9					8	1	
3		1				5		
		4		3			9	2
4	5	2	3	1	6		7	
		9	2					5
8				5	4	3	2	

GRID - 8

Hard

	6	4	5	2		8		9
		5			7	1		4
8		7		1		2		
5		1	6		9			
	8			3	5	7		6
6	7							1
3		6		5				8
	4				1		5	
9		2	3	8	4			

GRID - 1

Very Hard

	6	4	8		5	3	1	
5		8	6	1	2	7	9	
	2				7	8		6
		6	7					8
2					4	6		
4					6			5
		1	5		3		8	
8			9					
	5							1

GRID - 2

Very Hard

	3	1	9	8				5
8					4		2	
		2	1	7				
	4			5				9
			4	1	9	5		8
				3		7		
			8	9	1	3		
	9				3			1
	1				7	8		6

GRID - 3

Very Hard

					2		5	4
			7			1		3
6					1			
7	4		5	1			6	8
1		2			8	7	4	5
8	6	5					3	
4					3			
9	1		2			3		
			8			4		

GRID - 4

Very Hard

4	5	8	1	3		7	2	9
2					9			
	9	1		4				
			4				7	
				6	1	3	5	
			2	9	5			
5		4			7		9	
1	2						4	7
8	7	6		2	4	1	3	5

GRID - 5

Very Hard

4	8		7				6	9
		5		4	9			
3	1	9						
			9	3				
9		6		1			5	
					4	8		6
				2	3	9	7	
	9	8	1			4	3	
7		4				6		1

GRID - 6

Very Hard

						3		1
6			1			4	5	
3	2				5		7	
			2	8	4		3	
2			5					
		8						
5	4			1	7	9		
		3	4	9		5	6	7
9	7					1	4	2

You don't have to be great to start, but you have to start to be great. - Zig Ziglar

GRID - 7

Very Hard

		5	7	9				2
	4				1			
9		2	6			7		
				3				
7		8	9	6			4	1
						6	9	8
4		1		2		9		6
			1	7		8		4
6						1		5

GRID - 8

Very Hard

			7					
3	6	9	8			7		
7				9	6		4	
	8		4		2	5	6	
		2	9	5	3			8
					8	9		
1	3					4	5	
				4	5			
4	9	5						1

GRID - 5

Insane

				6	5			9
3	9				1			
	5					3	7	8
		5		4	8			2
		2		1				
9		1						
		3			9	2		
	6					7		
				7			9	4

GRID - 6

Insane

					4	9		5
	2		1					8
	1	4				3		
	7	8		2				
	5	6				2		4
		7	8	6		1		
			7				2	
	4	2	5				3	

GRID - 7

Insane

	8	9			7			1
			1					
						5		3
	4							
		7		8			9	6
1		8			3			
	5				4	8	6	
					8	1		
	1		5	2	9	4		

GRID - 8

Insane

		8	7				9	
	6					4		
							6	
8								7
	4			5			1	9
		5	1		7	8		
2	7				4			3
					2			
	9			1	8		7	2

MISSING VOWELS

A missing vowels puzzle is a word game that consists of the list of words where all vowels are removed (replaced by _ character).

The objective of this puzzle is to find and fill all the vowels hidden inside the words.

> Aromatherapy
>
> It helps reduce stress and anxiety by activating your senses and promoting relaxation. Choose a calming scent, such as lavender, peppermint, or chamomile. You can a scented candle or use an essential oil adding a few drops to a diffuser or a cotton ball. Inhale and smell a calming scent for 2-3 minutes.

Heart Health Words & Phrases 1

_g_

ST_M_

St_nt

G_nd_r

NST_M_

_b_s_ty

Sm_k_ng

_syst_l_

D__b_t_s

_x_rc_s_

_ng__gr_m

N_tr_t__n

P_ls_l_ss

M_d_c_t__n

_ng__pl_sty

Heart Health Words & Phrases 2

W__ght L_ss

C_rd__l_g_st

H__lthy D__t

H__rt _tt_ck

R_sk F_ct_rs

F_m_ly H_st_ry

_ng_n_ P_ct_r_s

H__rt Tr_nspl_nt

H_gh Ch_l_st_r_l

Phys_c_l Th_r_py

_l_ctr_c_rd__gr_m

L_f_styl_ Ch_ng_s

Sm_k_ng C_ss_t__n

Str_ss M_n_g_m_nt

V_lv_ R_pl_c_m_nt

Heart Health Words & Phrases 3

_p_n H__rt S_rg_ry

C_r_n_ry Thr_mb_s_s

H_gh Bl__d Pr_ss_r_

S_l_nt H__rt _tt_ck

_cc_p_t__n_l Th_r_py

My_c_rd__l _nf_rct__n

S_dd_n C_rd__c _rr_st

C_rd__c R_h_b_l_t_t__n

C_r_n_ry _rt_ry D_s__s_

V_ntr_c_l_r F_br_ll_t__n

C_r_n_ry _rt_ry Byp_ss Gr_ft_ng

P_rc_t_n___s C_r_n_ry _nt_rv_nt__n

WORD SCRAMBLE

Look carefully at the jumbled words and try unscrambling as many of the anagrams as you can into real words.

The jumbled words often have a theme which is dictated by each title.

> Visualisation
>
> It helps reduce stress and anxiety by creating a mental escape. Close your eyes and imagine yourself in a peaceful scene, such as a beach, a forest, or a mountain. Visualise all the details and the sensations, such as the sounds, smells, and textures. Use all your senses to imagine the scene for 2-3 minutes.

Australian Hospitals

OYALR LNEOBMRUE LPOHTAIS	
HTE RNIEPC ERSLACH ILPHTAOS	
TS NT'NCSVIE OPSATILH	
AONSMH DAIMCEL CEERNT	
NTISAU IHATPLOS RBIDGELEEH	
HET ELARFD	
NS'HDILREC IHLTPASO TA ETMSEADW	
TS TNNVI'CSE IEVTARP SPHOATLI STAE ORBUNLEEM	
OERPLVOIL TRAEH & TSCHE SPTAOHLI	
RLAYO NPCREI DRALFE OLATSIPH	
NYYEDS IAVSTTEND HPSATOLI	
WTESERN OAPHLITS	
TEH EELSWY ALITHOSP	
ORAYL BBAENRSI & 'OSNWME IALPHOTS	
EDSTEWMA POSHILAT	

Canadian Hospitals

RTNOOTO ALNEERG	
ONETMRLA EAGERNL PSTIAOLH	
MNOUT AINSI LPSTHAOI	
YNROUNKSOB LEHHAT CNESCISE TERNCE	
RVVEUACON ANLEGRE HPTAOLSI	
TS MLH'SEAIC OISHAPLT	
ERETNC IALOHIPETSR ED VNRSIUTEÉL'I ED MNATOLÉR	
EHWSIJ EREANLG PALITSOH	
GCMLLI TIENIYRSVU AHTHEL EERTNC	
NTHRO ORKY LNERGAE APILTSHO	
AOYLR IJEBEUL HPLAIOTS	
S.T AULSP' AILOTPSH	

The secret of change is to focus all of your energy, not on fighting the old, but on building the new. - Socrates

UK Hospitals

RLOAY MPTRBOON SLTHIOAP	
RGATE OMRODN SREETT HSTLIPOA	
NHJO CAFEFLRID HASTPILO	
'SKNIG GECLOLE OHPSLAIT	
YLARO TRHWPPOA IPALSHTO	
.ST BOMTERWHLA'OS OHISTAPL	
RLFEIAHED ATIOSHLP	
LEOOVIPLR EAHTR DNA TSHEC STOPLHIA	
YU'GS LOAPIHTS	
RAHICNG SCSRO OAPISTLH	
TS O'AHSTM SLOTPIHA	
BADDKR'OSEENO	
YSAWNTHEEHW IOHTSLPA	
MIEMSMHAHRT HOTSLIPA	
AYRLO EERF HPTSIOAL	
NODGLE JIUEELB ANOTNALI IALSTPOH	
RYOAL RYMNFIRIA FO RUIENGHDB TA LLTIET REFANC	
DORIRDREF PATLSOHI	

US Hospitals

VNLALDCEE ILICCN	
OYMA LICNCI	
EHTTCAASSUSMS RNLGAEE PALTSHIO	
TEH HOSJN HKOINPS OLPTHIAS	
HTE UTOMN NISIA LSPHOAIT	
ARHIBMG DNA NME'OSW HPAISLTO	
ENW YOKR ESBPTINRAYER HISOPALT	
LABORY TS E'UKSL MACELID CNREET	
DRSECA NIAIS EALDMIC CNTEER	
OFRSANTD ITLSAPHO	
UNY NOALEGN IOPSTLAHS	
UEDK TIVNYSUIRE AIPSOTLH	
ULCA EHHTAL – ONLRAD GRNEAA LMCDAIE ENRETC	
NTNEERTRHSWO MLOREIMA HILATPSO	
HIPASTLO FO ETH TENSRIIVYU FO EYSAPLNNNAIV	
TONOUSH MSHOETTID HPOSLITA	
IVRNUIESYT FO AICCOHG MCELAID ETRCEN	
NOBOTS LRNESICHD ISAOLHTP	
USFC LAEICMD RCTNEE	
IIRNTYSVEU FO INICGMHA ISAOPHLT	

WORDSEARCH

A word game that consists of the letters of words placed in a grid.

The objective of this puzzle is to find and mark all the words hidden inside the box. The words may be placed horizontally, vertically, backwards or diagonally.

A list of the hidden words is provided, but more challenging puzzles may not provide a list.

> *Gratitude Practice*
>
> *It helps shift your focus from negative to positive and improves your overall wellbeing. It helps to focus on positive things and increases overall happiness. Grab a notebook and pen, and write down 3 things you're grateful for today. They can be small or big things, such as a good cup of coffee, a beautiful sunrise, sunshine or your loved ones.*

WORDS OF WELLBEING 1

J	N	R	F	M	L	V	X	Y	T	D	T	W	N	J	E	I	T	W	D
V	X	B	I	T	A	M	M	E	C	K	S	Z	O	X	H	Z	J	T	F
T	A	X	C	X	G	I	F	J	G	N	E	X	E	R	B	G	G	M	Z
X	W	E	K	L	O	D	P	T	N	B	R	R	I	I	K	E	O	J	N
R	E	K	A	M	M	V	P	R	M	A	C	N	B	O	T	O	M	Y	T
N	L	A	W	E	T	T	M	M	E	I	C	K	A	H	Z	K	U	T	A
T	L	T	S	P	Z	Y	G	E	S	D	H	R	F	L	W	W	G	T	H
M	N	N	Y	A	P	N	N	E	C	L	O	E	D	P	T	N	B	I	I
E	E	I	B	T	W	S	U	O	W	K	Z	L	T	E	O	B	A	L	E
Q	S	R	G	D	I	E	K	T	I	D	I	A	G	P	E	E	L	S	M
C	S	E	C	Z	R	V	C	Q	R	T	K	X	S	H	R	K	M	A	T
S	P	T	Z	Y	H	T	I	D	H	I	A	A	F	L	N	W	N	D	F
M	S	A	P	C	L	W	D	T	P	L	T	T	F	Y	I	I	O	E	B
X	S	W	X	K	R	R	E	O	C	B	A	I	I	L	V	Q	I	H	A
F	I	T	N	E	S	S	E	K	A	A	I	O	O	D	G	M	T	Z	C
Z	R	C	S	R	D	X	C	Y	A	D	T	N	Z	N	E	W	A	C	B
P	A	L	G	D	L	V	I	L	W	A	K	H	Y	Z	P	M	R	Z	I
D	E	Q	G	N	I	T	A	E	Y	H	T	L	A	E	H	V	D	W	V
X	G	S	T	N	E	M	E	L	P	P	U	S	L	Y	M	T	Y	T	I
O	C	E	M	V	Q	V	I	T	A	M	I	N	S	H	A	E	H	K	A

Activity	Meditation	Supplements
Exercise	Nutrition	Vitamins
Fitness	Relaxation	Water Intake
Healthy Eating	Rest	Wellness
Hydration	Sleep	Workout

WORDS OF WELLBEING 2

Y	P	W	Y	X	I	J	K	W	X	E	M	B	S	A	Q	W	C	H	B
T	R	R	Q	S	K	G	K	Y	T	I	L	I	B	I	X	E	L	F	E
E	I	M	M	U	N	I	T	Y	N	F	D	N	Q	H	T	L	A	E	H
C	S	N	R	P	B	S	K	H	O	M	E	G	B	K	Q	F	F	E	V
N	C	L	E	A	N	S	I	N	G	G	T	S	Z	D	X	F	E	I	P
A	H	G	C	C	N	L	Y	H	W	Z	O	X	I	B	K	W	Y	O	G
L	C	T	O	I	K	W	C	I	X	L	X	R	R	Q	T	K	G	K	O
A	H	G	V	Q	P	R	E	V	E	N	T	I	O	N	S	T	P	I	J
B	D	Y	E	P	Q	E	Y	N	R	Y	O	I	H	O	W	H	V	T	G
Z	F	E	R	O	P	O	G	T	C	N	M	Y	T	E	I	X	N	A	A
K	X	T	Y	R	X	C	M	Y	I	R	X	G	C	V	V	K	W	Y	H
I	Z	N	S	T	S	V	D	J	M	L	O	H	H	Q	S	T	P	I	E
J	G	A	Q	R	I	Q	S	A	Y	S	I	P	W	H	H	X	E	F	A
E	C	N	A	T	S	I	S	E	R	W	T	B	C	H	W	B	R	B	L
J	F	Q	A	V	O	I	D	A	N	C	E	R	A	G	T	K	Q	T	I
R	X	D	M	S	T	Y	J	F	W	X	G	K	E	T	V	Z	T	H	N
F	F	E	Q	U	I	L	I	B	R	I	U	M	D	S	P	H	G	K	G
P	Y	K	J	S	M	N	J	X	K	E	A	Q	K	W	S	A	S	M	V
A	R	R	J	J	Z	O	H	X	F	X	G	R	Y	R	C	I	D	K	H
V	L	S	V	S	Z	F	G	S	T	Y	J	E	Q	Z	N	R	I	A	D

Adaptability	Detox	Immunity
Anxiety	Equilibrium	Prevention
Avoidance	Flexibility	Recovery
Balance	Healing	Resistance
Cleansing	Health	Stress

WORDS OF WELLBEING 3

A	C	C	Q	G	N	I	N	A	E	M	Q	W	F	Y	L	V	L	P	Z
C	O	Y	M	K	K	K	M	D	I	D	V	P	G	Q	L	N	J	X	K
C	A	S	Q	J	V	Q	K	S	Y	N	O	I	T	C	E	N	N	O	C
E	N	N	G	O	Q	I	G	P	D	N	G	J	X	Q	P	L	W	T	C
P	Q	R	V	S	Y	A	F	R	S	Y	I	A	N	X	D	P	Z	X	S
T	G	E	M	M	L	P	F	B	G	X	O	O	K	M	N	J	X	D	I
A	V	D	K	L	X	K	E	N	D	U	R	A	N	C	E	M	T	Z	H
N	Q	U	J	F	O	R	T	I	T	U	D	E	O	Q	B	O	R	G	Q
C	H	T	K	A	N	I	M	A	T	S	Z	K	R	N	Y	M	W	F	S
E	B	I	P	M	S	I	I	L	D	K	X	V	H	J	E	E	J	M	R
L	L	T	J	N	P	N	Q	I	D	H	Z	C	C	N	L	N	Q	L	Z
F	O	A	B	W	L	N	Z	L	N	W	T	K	T	S	C	C	S	Z	C
S	V	R	O	S	B	M	A	M	S	P	Z	A	Q	I	T	Z	Q	P	V
O	E	G	J	N	P	T	D	O	R	S	L	H	L	Y	I	X	L	J	J
H	K	P	H	Y	S	I	C	A	L	B	L	A	N	O	I	T	O	M	E
F	K	V	G	G	Q	E	G	A	R	U	O	C	K	L	G	V	H	L	K
I	X	F	I	K	S	Y	N	N	G	G	W	A	D	V	B	T	D	O	H
O	I	Z	G	F	S	R	E	S	I	L	I	E	N	C	E	J	P	S	Q
X	C	F	R	E	S	O	P	R	U	P	S	X	H	A	N	W	L	P	Z
M	S	I	M	I	T	P	O	O	Y	M	L	M	L	N	F	B	F	X	J

Acceptance	Fortitude	Optimism
Connection	Gratitude	Physical
Courage	Love	Purpose
Emotional	Meaning	Resilience
Endurance	Mental	Stamina

WORDS OF WELLBEING 4

H	I	J	K	M	H	W	B	J	A	R	P	H	T	P	L	S	Y	P	S
P	H	I	P	E	F	N	O	C	M	E	R	A	C	F	L	E	S	P	E
F	H	C	Y	R	Q	M	U	X	V	D	R	O	T	D	B	J	K	L	L
G	T	R	S	T	Y	O	N	A	P	X	D	N	M	Q	A	X	R	A	F
N	G	E	L	L	M	P	D	G	C	G	E	Y	L	B	B	K	M	Y	A
I	N	A	J	X	C	O	A	V	K	M	M	X	A	J	O	Y	D	F	W
H	G	T	P	V	C	K	R	C	T	Z	L	B	C	B	R	G	R	U	A
S	J	I	L	Z	L	R	I	N	N	Y	X	G	F	T	P	M	T	L	R
I	I	V	H	V	N	S	E	C	N	A	D	N	U	B	A	C	I	N	E
R	Q	I	T	H	T	T	S	X	E	W	K	P	P	P	R	O	D	E	N
U	J	T	E	F	N	F	P	Q	S	N	E	G	B	X	M	N	Z	S	E
O	N	Y	R	O	Y	X	M	V	F	F	V	Z	C	T	O	F	T	S	S
L	O	P	C	O	G	C	N	D	R	R	X	A	Y	X	C	M	Q	R	S
F	X	Y	H	T	A	P	M	E	G	C	V	V	K	N	Y	B	Z	N	L
L	K	N	D	J	P	G	R	A	C	E	M	W	H	H	S	M	N	J	X
K	E	A	Q	E	K	W	Q	L	F	L	B	B	Y	Y	K	P	W	J	T
H	W	B	A	L	D	C	I	K	H	V	L	R	V	S	Z	F	H	V	V
A	K	C	I	N	O	I	S	S	A	P	M	O	C	F	L	E	S	Q	Z
N	E	R	I	D	I	R	P	P	T	N	E	M	L	L	I	F	L	U	F
N	R	J	D	J	Z	L	C	M	Z	E	X	H	Y	L	C	O	X	F	I

Abundance
Boundaries
Calm
Contentment
Creativity
Empathy
Flourishing
Fulfillment
Grace
Joy
Peace
Playfulness
Self-awareness
Self-care
Self-compassion

WORDS OF WELLBEING 5

P	Z	G	M	S	I	A	V	Z	O	B	O	C	Y	V	Y	M	T	S	E
E	O	D	I	I	N	M	W	S	J	E	I	L	E	J	J	R	Q	E	G
A	I	N	V	G	N	T	A	S	F	T	Y	D	E	O	O	Q	O	H	H
C	D	I	P	M	Z	D	J	S	R	W	L	C	J	Y	L	N	Z	O	S
E	Y	M	Y	V	H	B	F	A	S	T	B	E	C	F	A	H	N	M	M
F	G	A	J	W	S	W	N	U	P	A	K	L	L	U	T	E	N	Q	L
U	T	T	E	X	P	Q	D	R	L	F	G	R	D	L	Y	G	P	M	C
L	A	I	D	D	U	T	O	Y	B	N	R	E	I	N	R	O	L	A	V
N	E	V	Y	I	F	T	Z	J	I	F	E	J	G	E	M	X	C	H	J
E	N	E	L	Y	E	L	M	B	F	Q	W	S	Q	S	F	B	C	B	D
S	D	I	Z	I	I	D	N	Q	P	Y	S	V	S	S	Q	O	Q	E	D
S	T	C	N	X	Q	I	Y	S	A	C	X	X	P	Q	B	G	T	E	N
Y	B	M	I	N	S	P	I	R	A	T	I	O	N	O	P	O	P	Y	S
L	K	G	R	P	N	D	L	N	M	S	E	I	L	M	X	O	R	B	H
Y	C	W	Z	G	L	F	X	V	V	W	Z	Q	M	Q	H	D	T	L	V
W	Y	T	F	W	K	O	E	W	D	E	X	O	G	I	E	V	N	I	M
T	A	R	A	S	V	X	Q	P	Z	E	N	L	W	T	C	Q	I	C	C
K	C	M	Y	Z	O	G	C	Y	T	I	N	A	S	T	I	K	W	C	J
C	W	A	A	Z	I	N	A	I	R	A	T	E	G	E	V	V	Q	V	H
R	R	Z	E	O	Z	K	S	N	F	Y	M	Y	A	G	O	Y	L	N	W

Detox	Massage	Tranquility
Honey	Mindfulness	Vegetarian
Hope	Peacefulness	Vitamin
Inspiration	Protein	Yoga
Joyfulness	Sanity	Zen

COLOURING

Colouring is for more than children. It calms the brain and helps your body relax. Colouring can be beneficial for sleep and fatigue while decreasing body aches, heart rate, respiration, and feelings of depression and anxiety. It helps relax your brain and improves brain and motor functions.

Whether you colour just for fun or to relax your mind, there's no reason you shouldn't try it. The next time you're feeling overwhelmed, take your mind off of the problem and start colouring.

"

Practice Self-Compassion
It can help reduce stress and improve overall well-being. Self-compassion involves treating yourself with kindness and understanding. Take a moment to acknowledge your feelings and offer yourself words of comfort and support.

"

Don't think
it's too late
but keep
working on it

Your presence can
give happiness
I hope you
remember that

Life isn't about
being perfect
it's about
accomplishing
your dreams

GAMES TO PLAY WITH FRIENDS

Sometimes I found that when I had visitors, I would run out of things to talk about. Being in hospital or recovering at home isn't the most exciting life to have lots to say about. Here are some puzzles that you can play together with your friends and family.

Tic Tac Toe
The game is played on a grid that's 9 squares. You are X, the other player is O. Each player takes turns putting their marks in empty squares.

The first player to get 3 of their marks in a row (up, down, across, or diagonally) is the winner. When all 9 squares are full, the game is over.

Hangman
One person, the 'host' chooses a word and marks the length of the word on the grid. The other player has to guess the letters in this word/phrase before all the parts of the hangman are drawn.

If the player guesses correctly the letter is marked in the correct place, if the player guesses incorrectly the host draws another part of the hangman.

The game continues until the word/phrase is guessed (all letters are revealed) in this case the second person has won. If all the parts of the hangman are displayed in this case the second person has lost.

Four In a Row
Each of the players choose a colour pen or pencil and then take turns 'dropping' coloured discs by highlighting a circle on the game.

The two players alternate turns dropping one of their discs at a time into a column, until one of the players achieves a column, row or diagonal four in a row, and wins the game.

Don't watch the clock; do what it does. Keep going. - Sam Levenson

"Take a walk
Taking a walk can help improve circulation, reduce stress and increase energy. It can help you relax and clear your mind. Go for a walk in your neighbourhood or a nearby park for 10 minutes. Whilst walking look at the tops of the trees or the chimney pots, raising your posture also helps you feel good too."

TIC TAC TOE

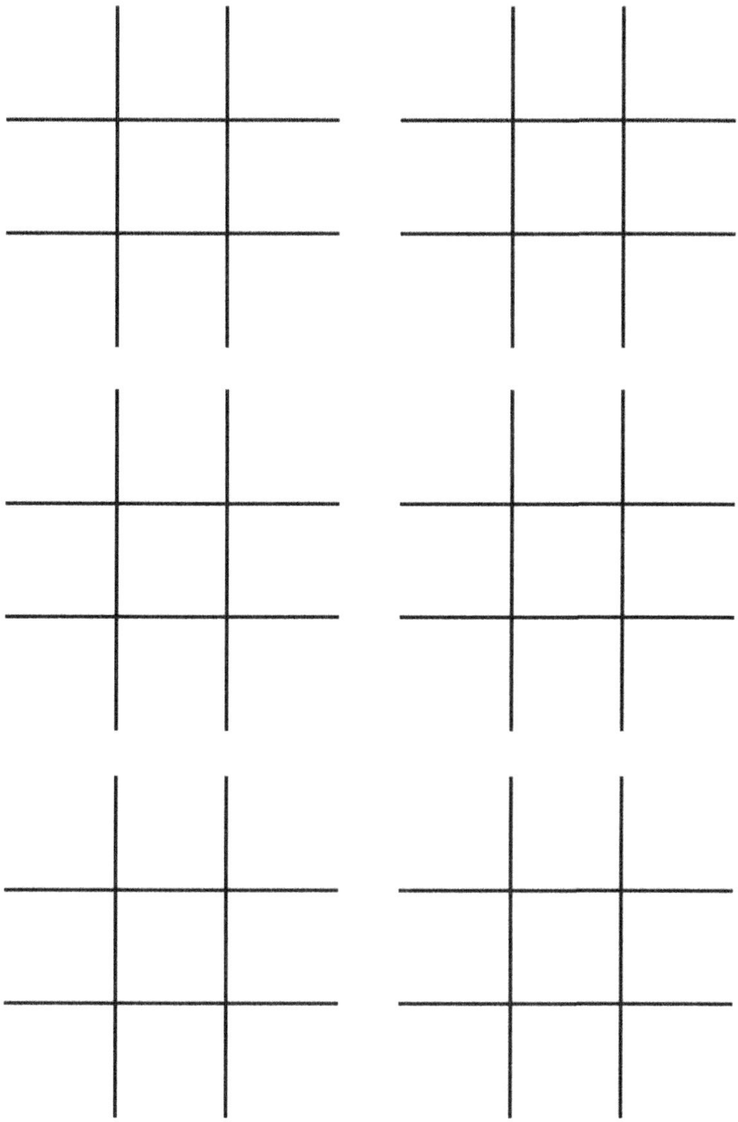

TIC TAC TOE

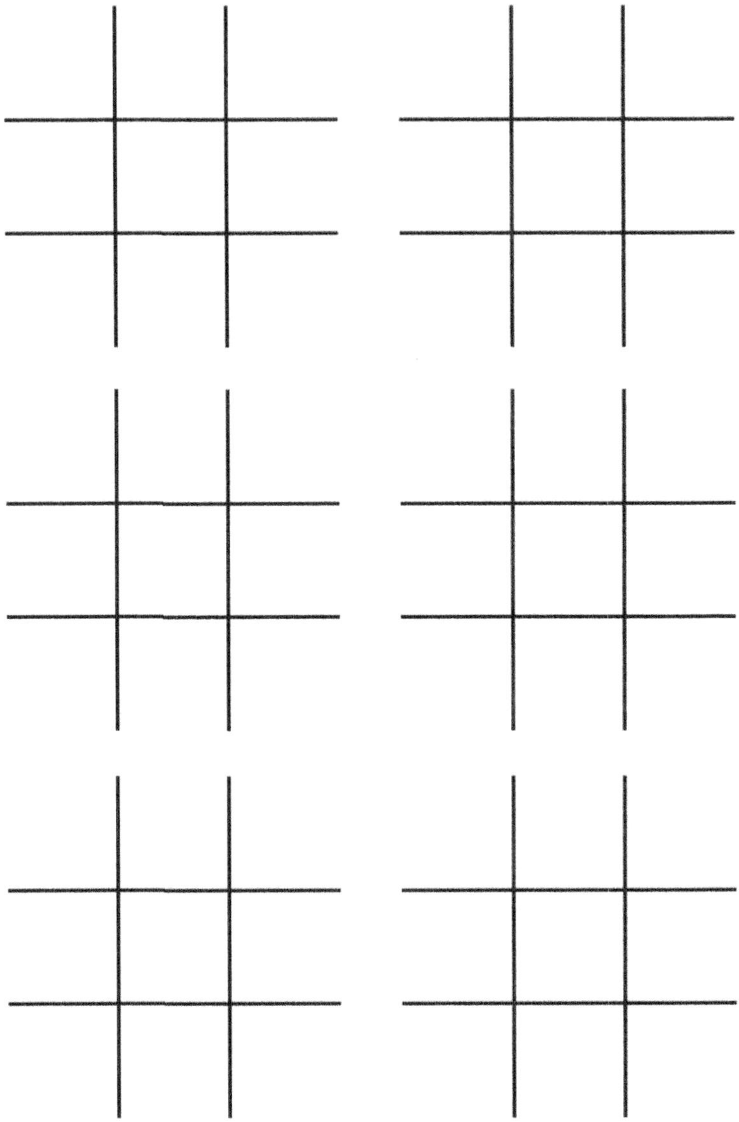

HANGMAN

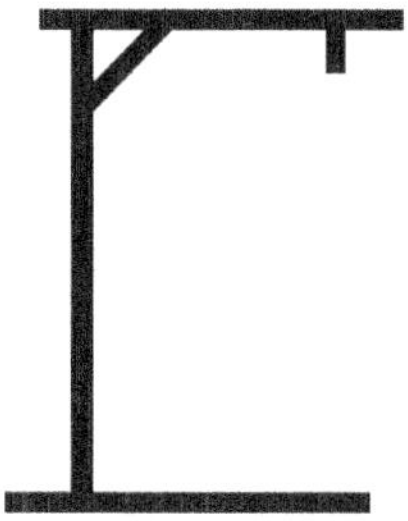

Word: ____________________

A B C D E F G H I J K L M N
O P Q R S T U V W X Y Z

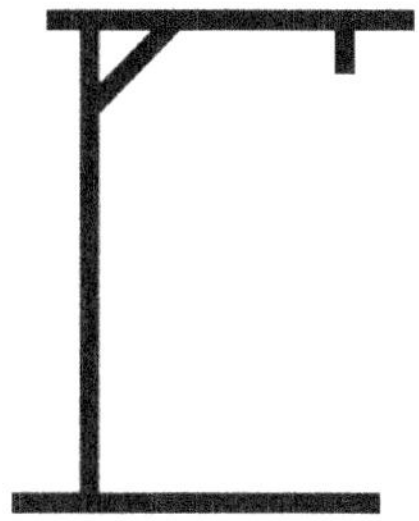

Word: ____________________

A B C D E F G H I J K L M N
O P Q R S T U V W X Y Z

Word: ____________________

A B C D E F G H I J K L M N
O P Q R S T U V W X Y Z

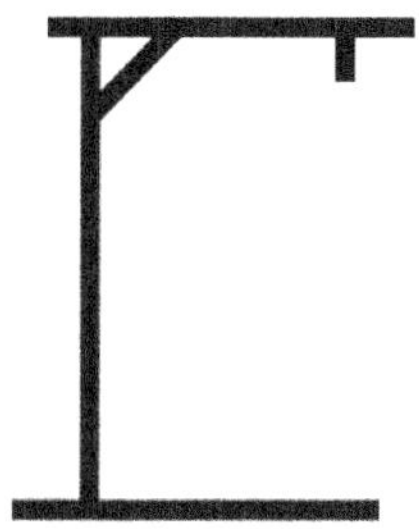

Word: ____________________

A B C D E F G H I J K L M N
O P Q R S T U V W X Y Z

HANGMAN

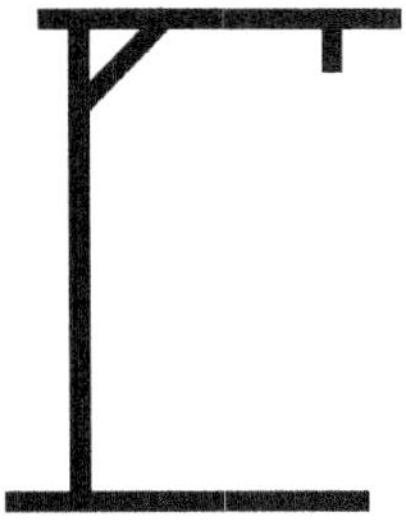

Word: ____________________

A B C D E F G H I J K L M N
O P Q R S T U V W X Y Z

Word: ____________________

A B C D E F G H I J K L M N
O P Q R S T U V W X Y Z

Word: ____________________

A B C D E F G H I J K L M N
O P Q R S T U V W X Y Z

Word: ____________________

A B C D E F G H I J K L M N
O P Q R S T U V W X Y Z

FOUR IN A ROW

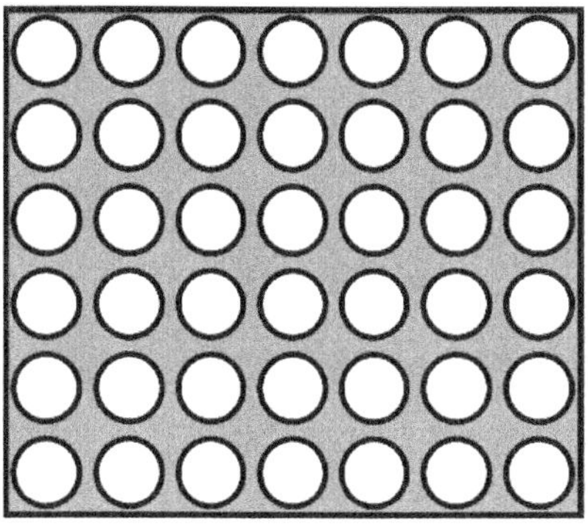

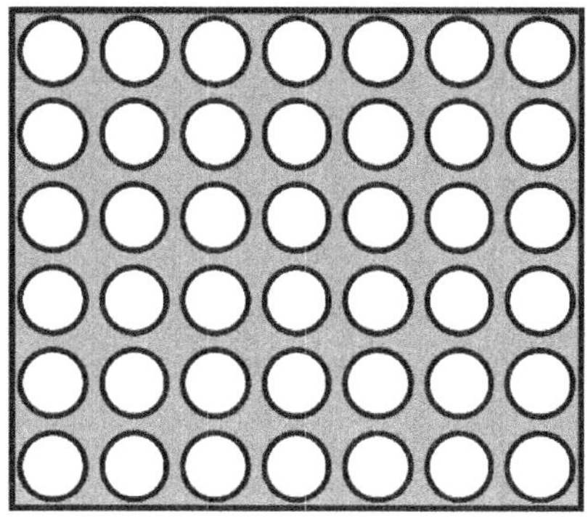

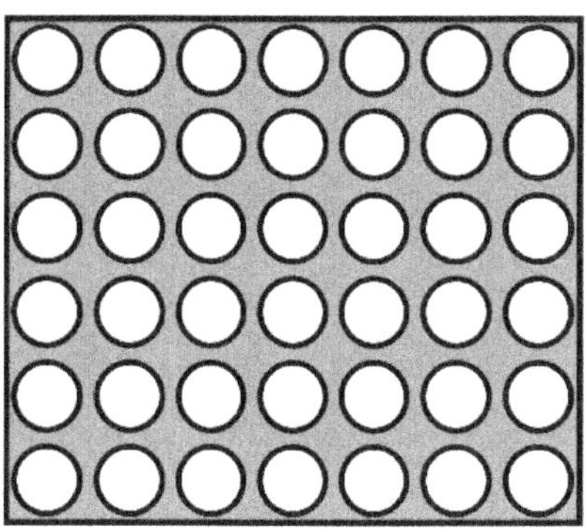

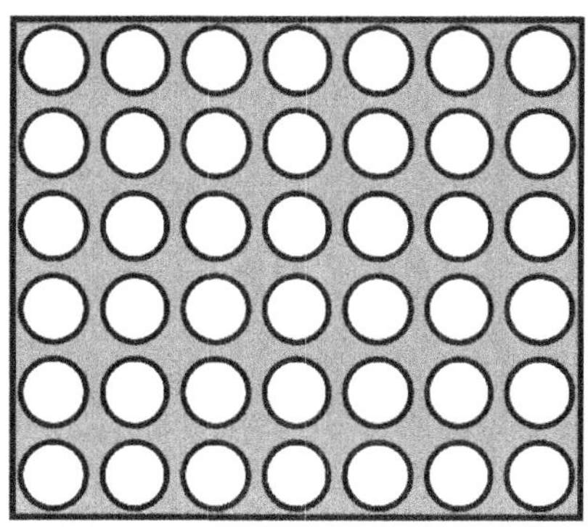

FOUR IN A ROW

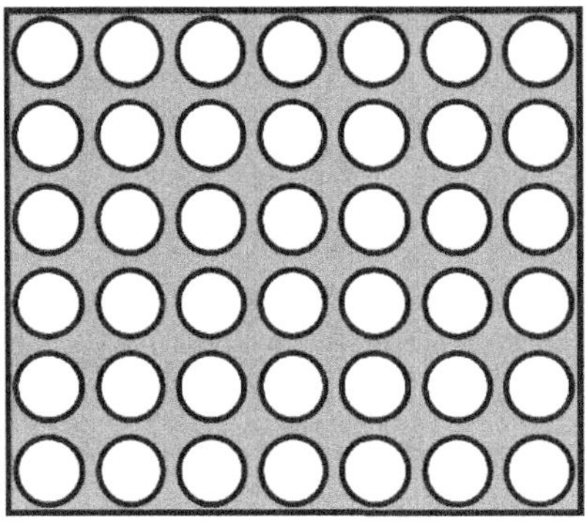

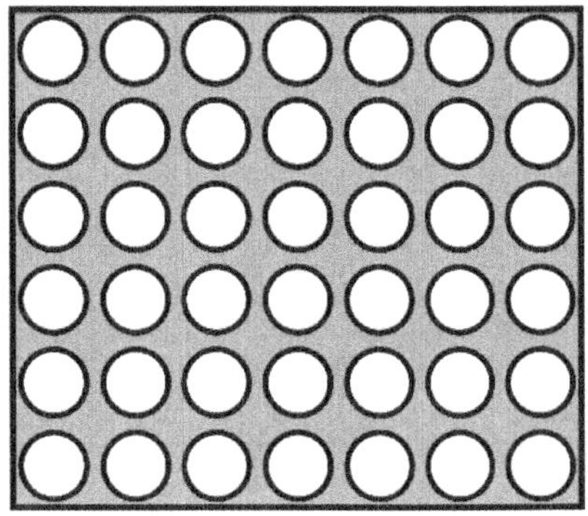

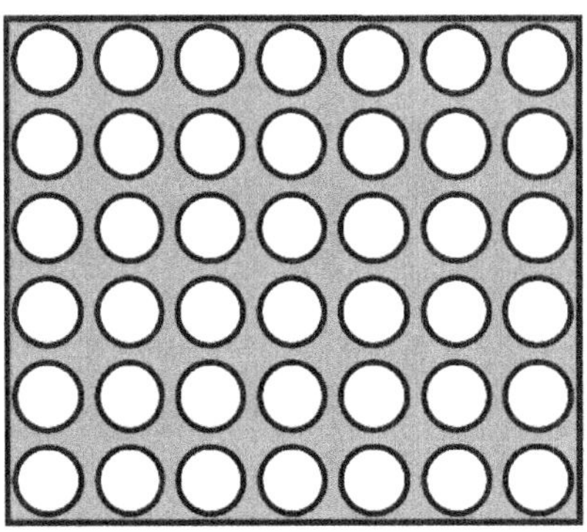

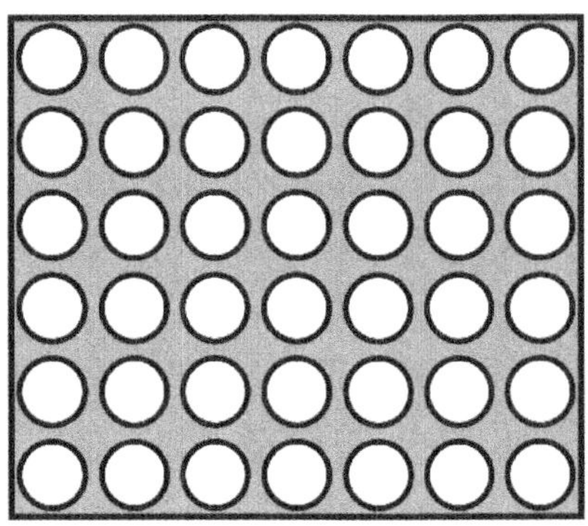

SOLUTIONS

If you are enjoying this book, please leave a review on Amazon. It would mean a lot to me!

You don't have to be great to start, but you have to start to be great. - Zig Ziglar

> “ Music Therapy
> It helps reduce stress and anxiety by slowing breathing and heart rate and helps improve your mood. Find a quiet place, put on some headphones, and listen to calming music for 10 minutes. Alternatively boost your mood by finding an up-tempo song that you love and listen to it for a few minutes. Sing along or tap your feet to the beat. ”

Lifestyle Changes 1

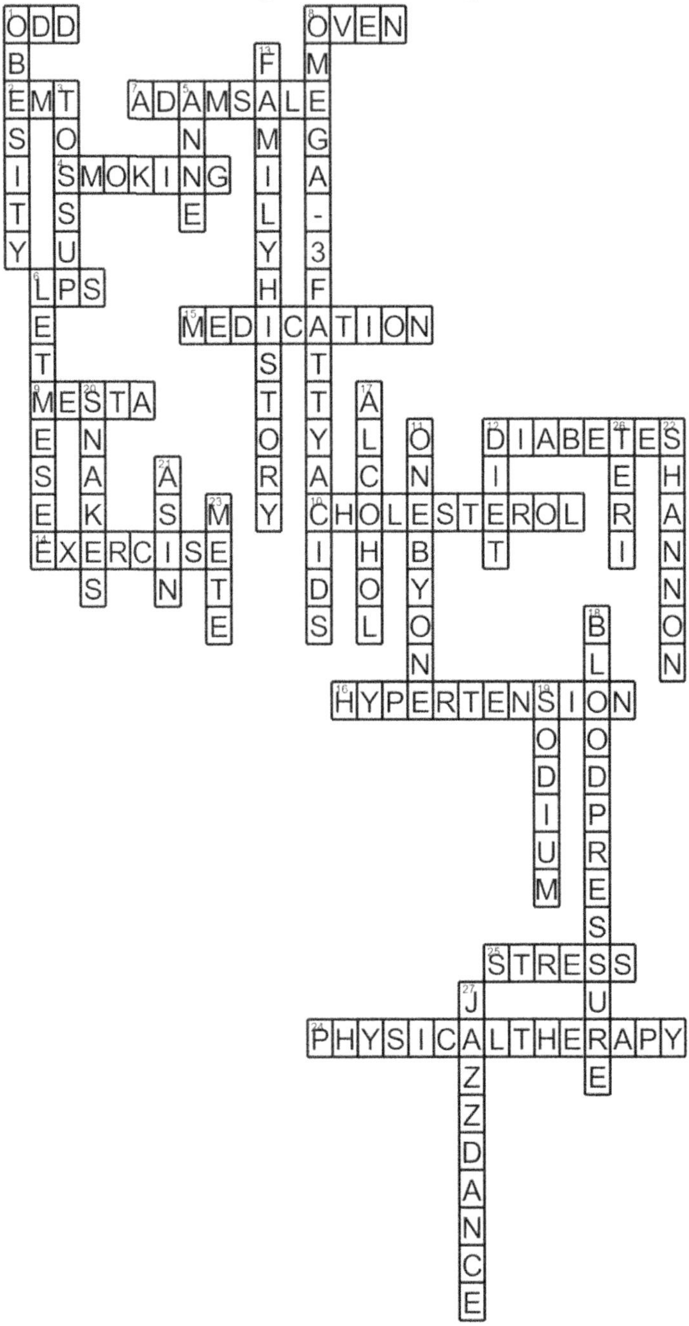

Cardiac Medications 1

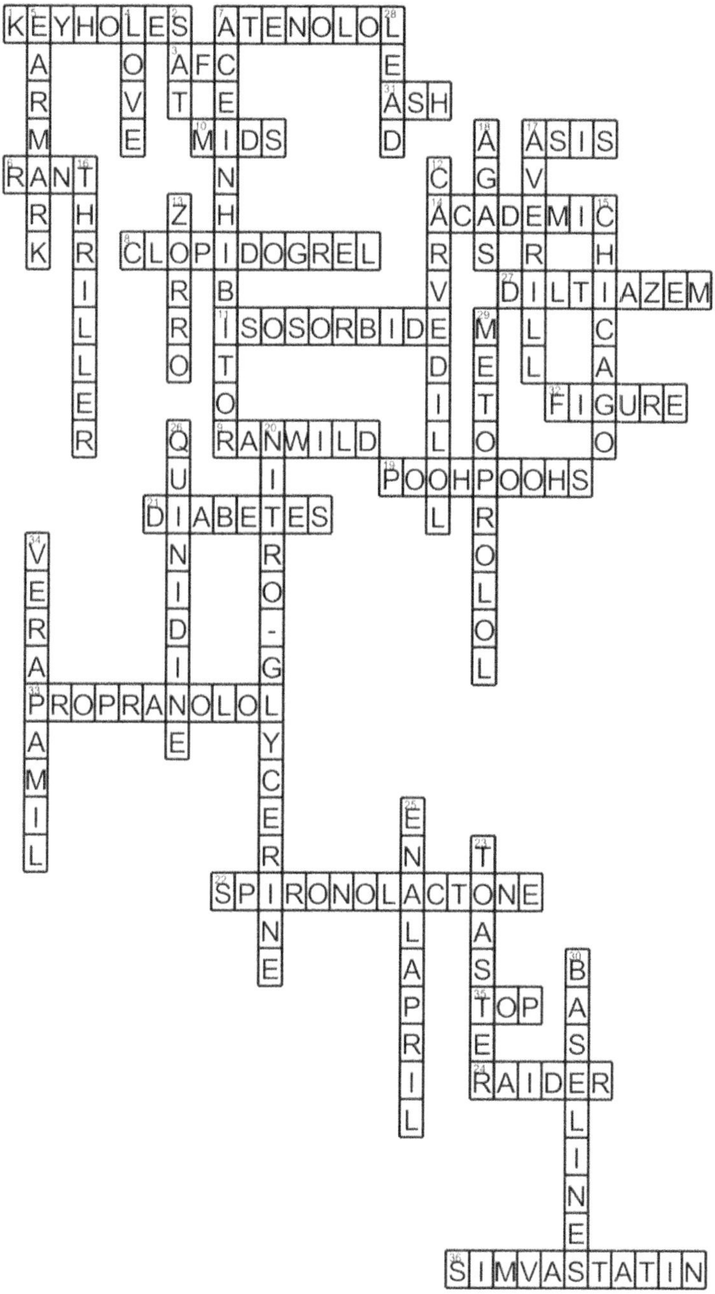

Psychological Therapies

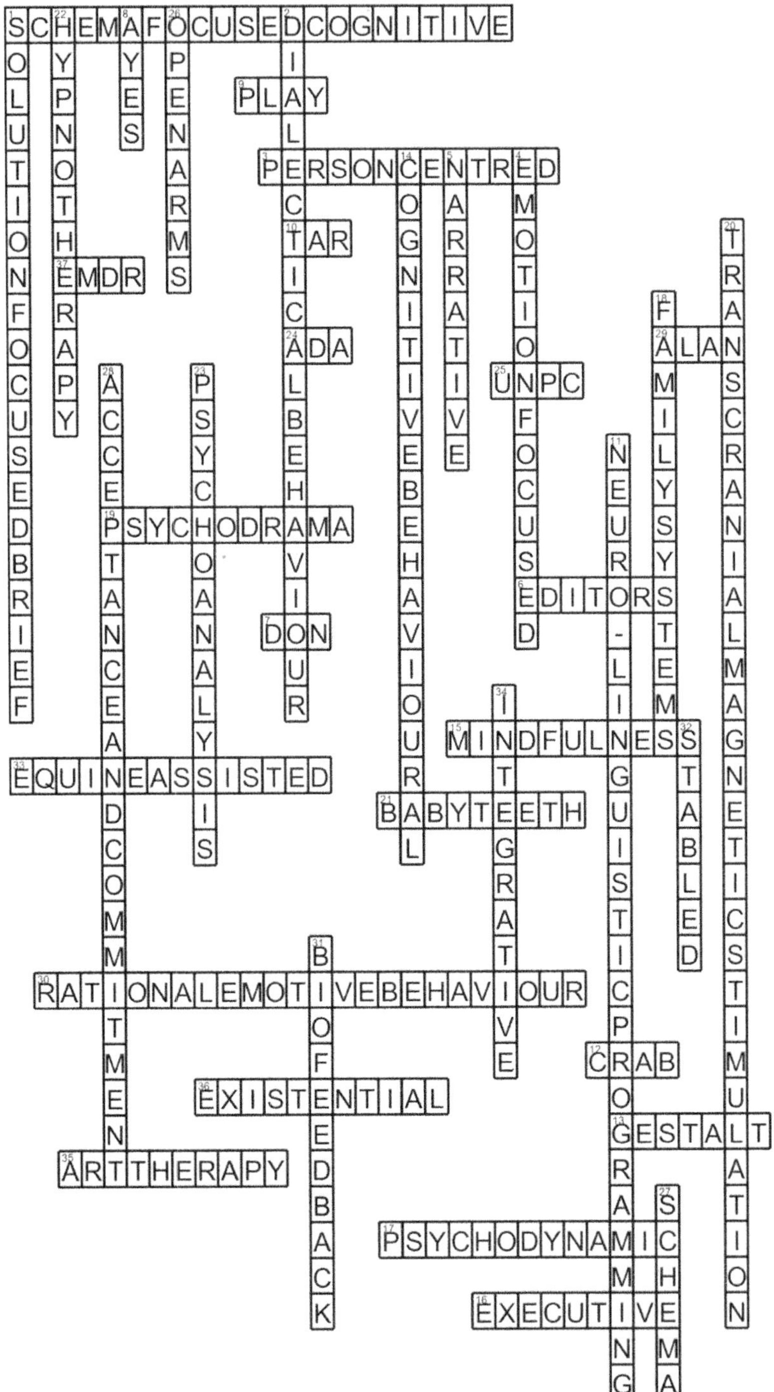

Cardiac Terminology 1

Hospital Related

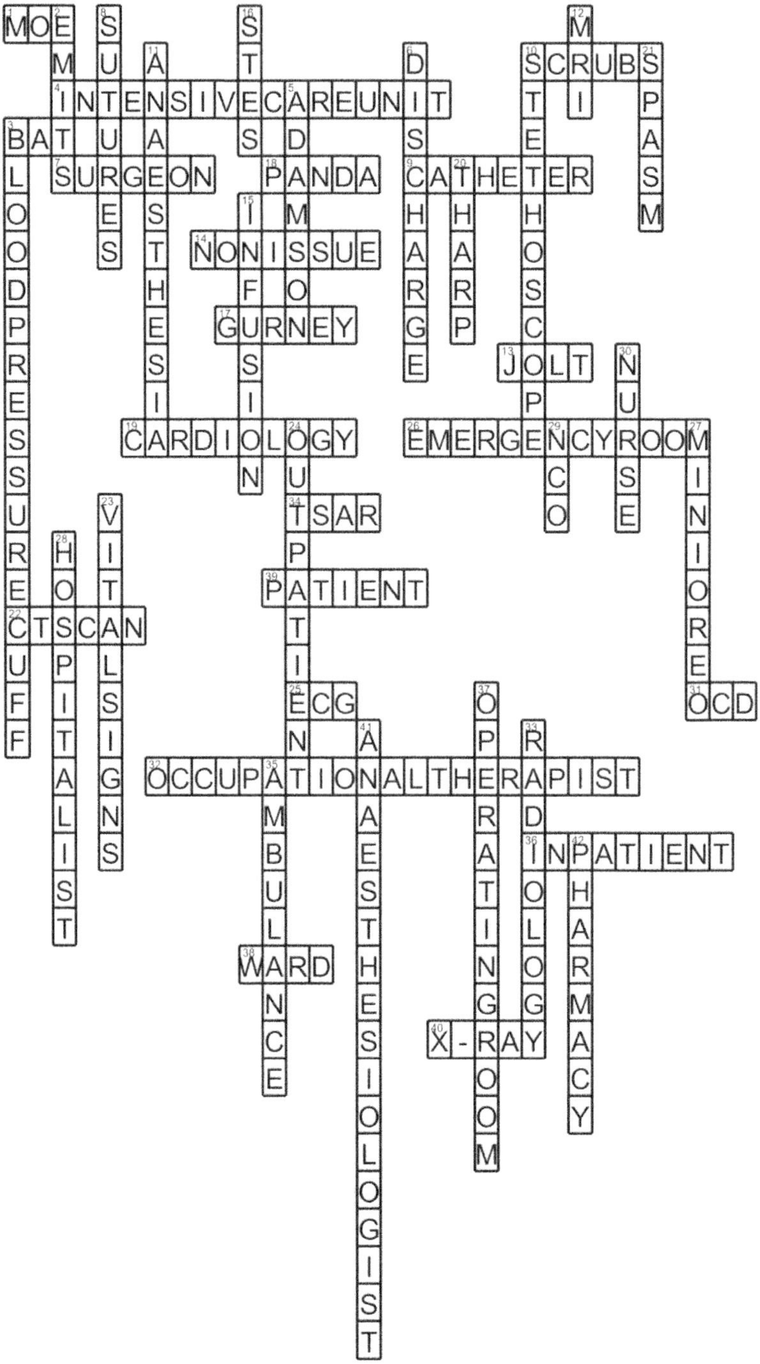

Exercise & Activity

Parts of the Heart 1

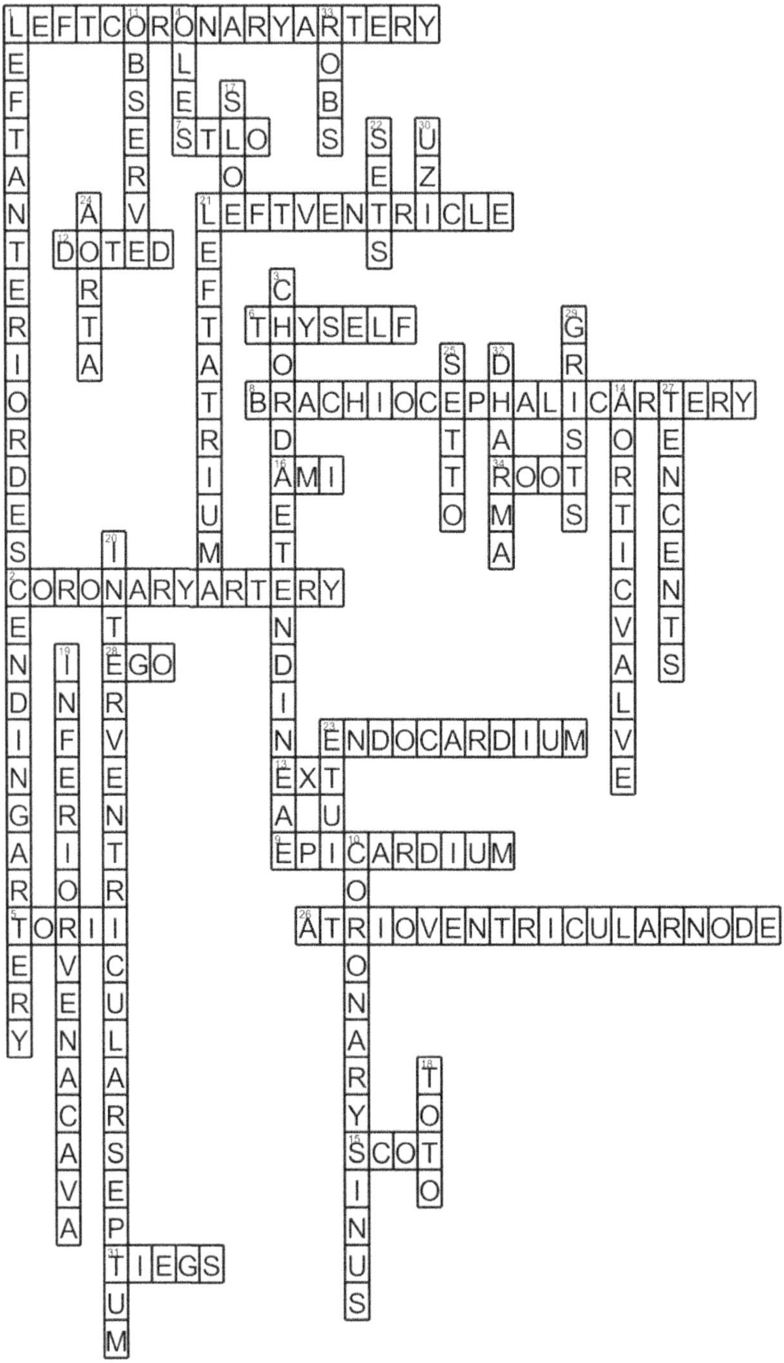

Cardiac Terminology 2

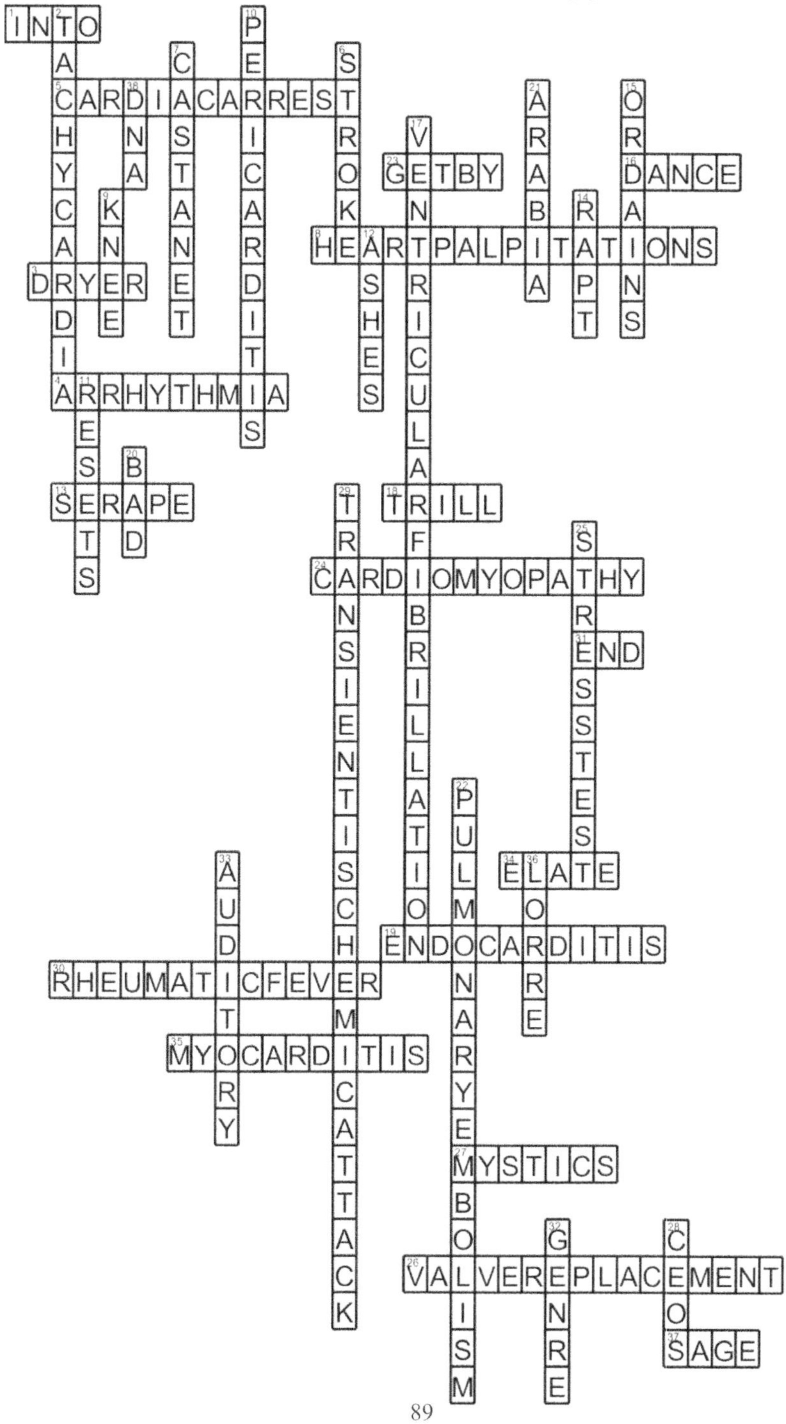

Cardiology Team

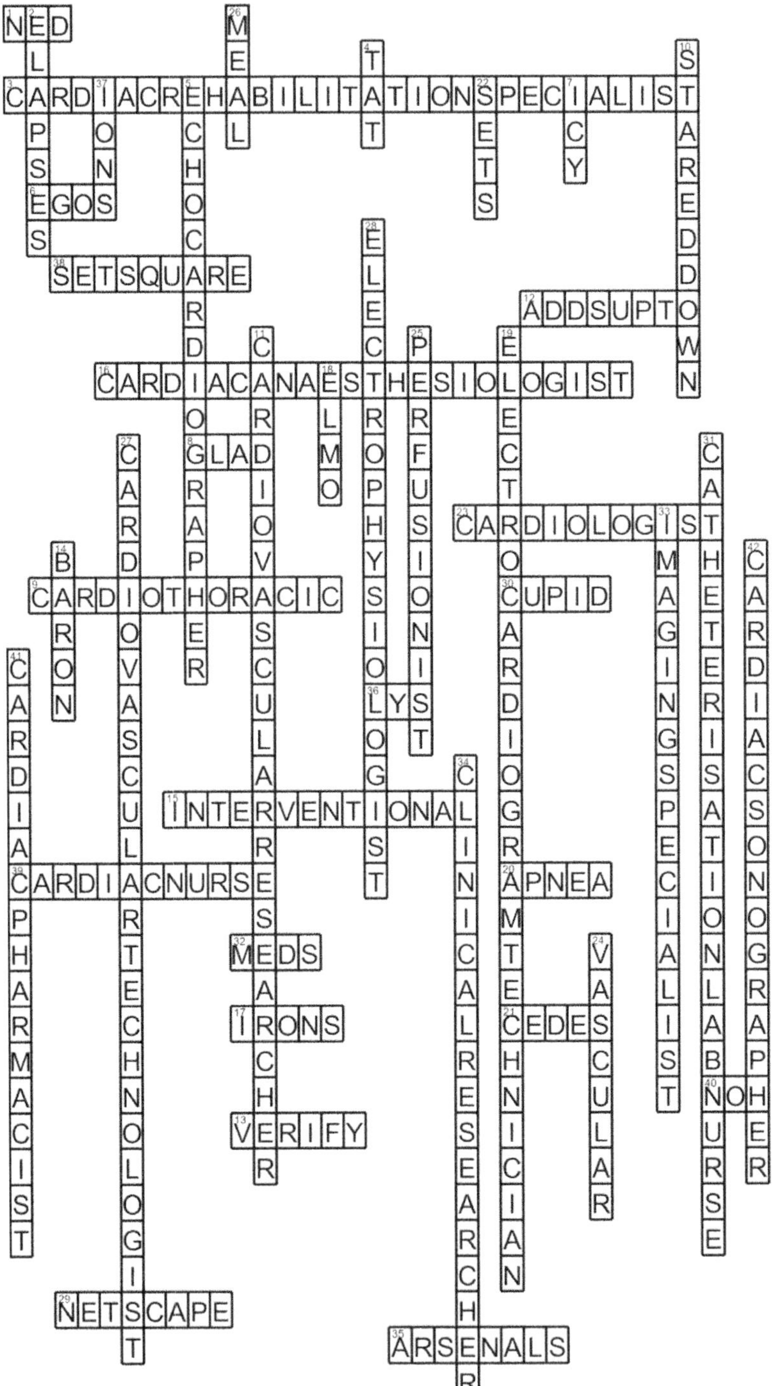

Investigations & Tests 1

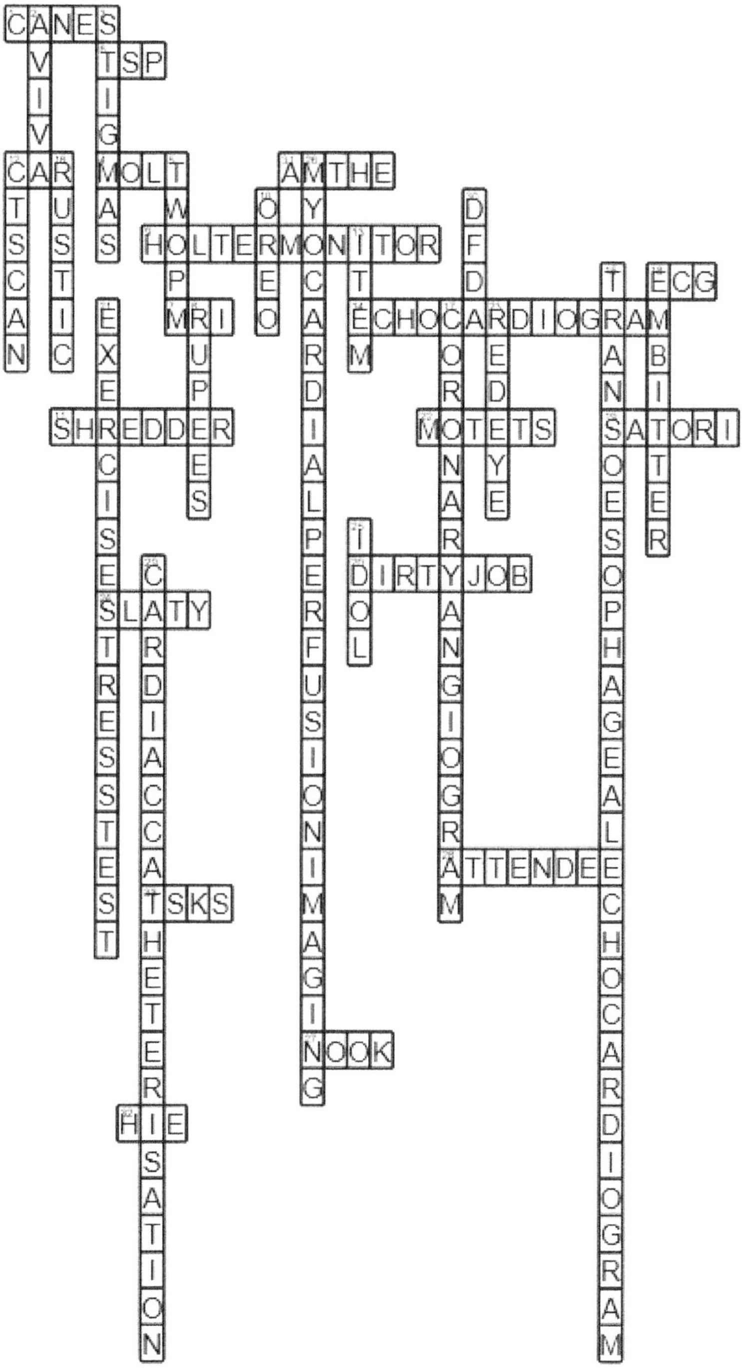

Lifestyle Changes 2

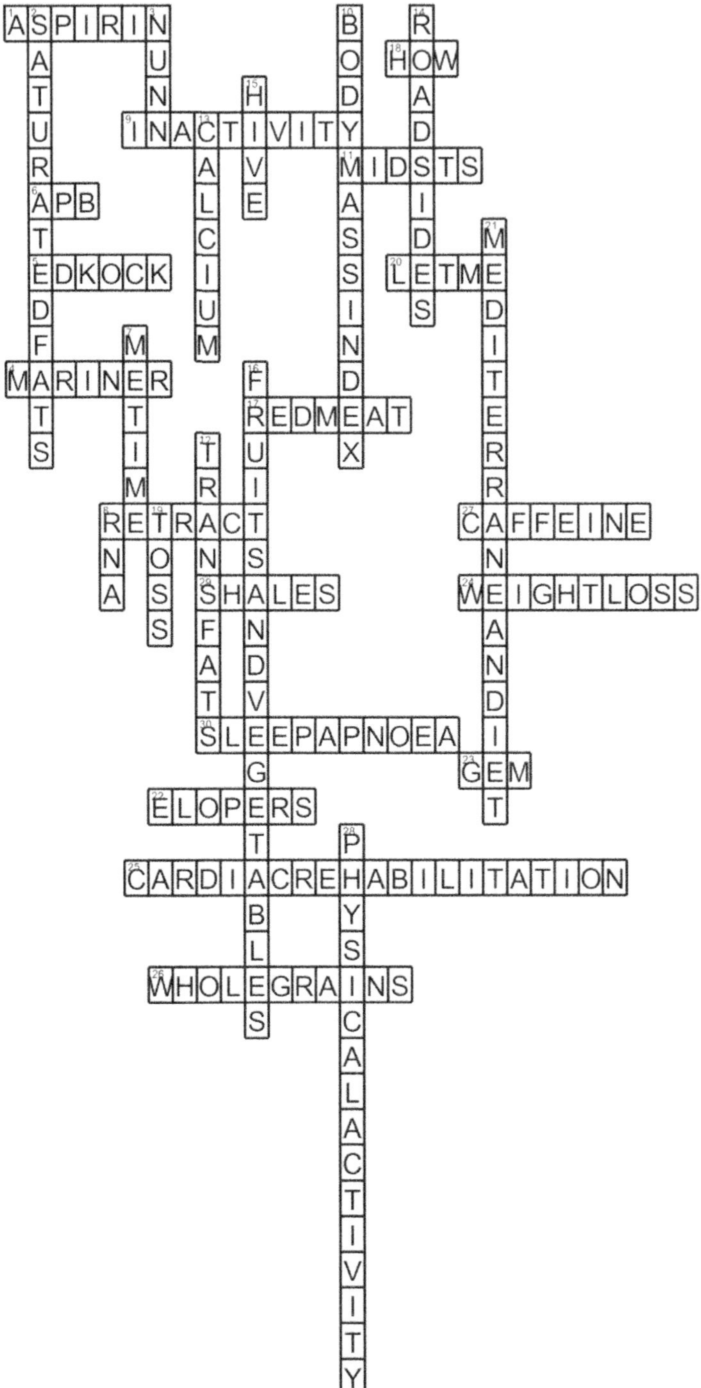

Heart Healthy Food

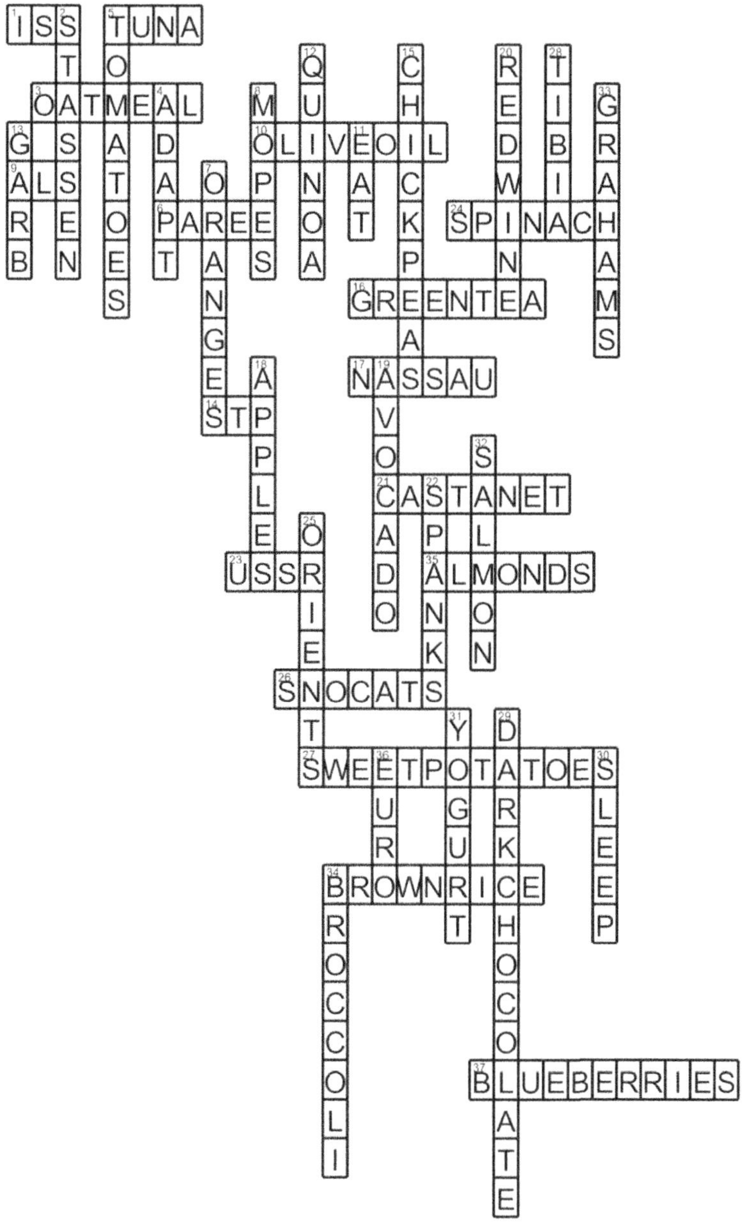

Parts of the Heart 2

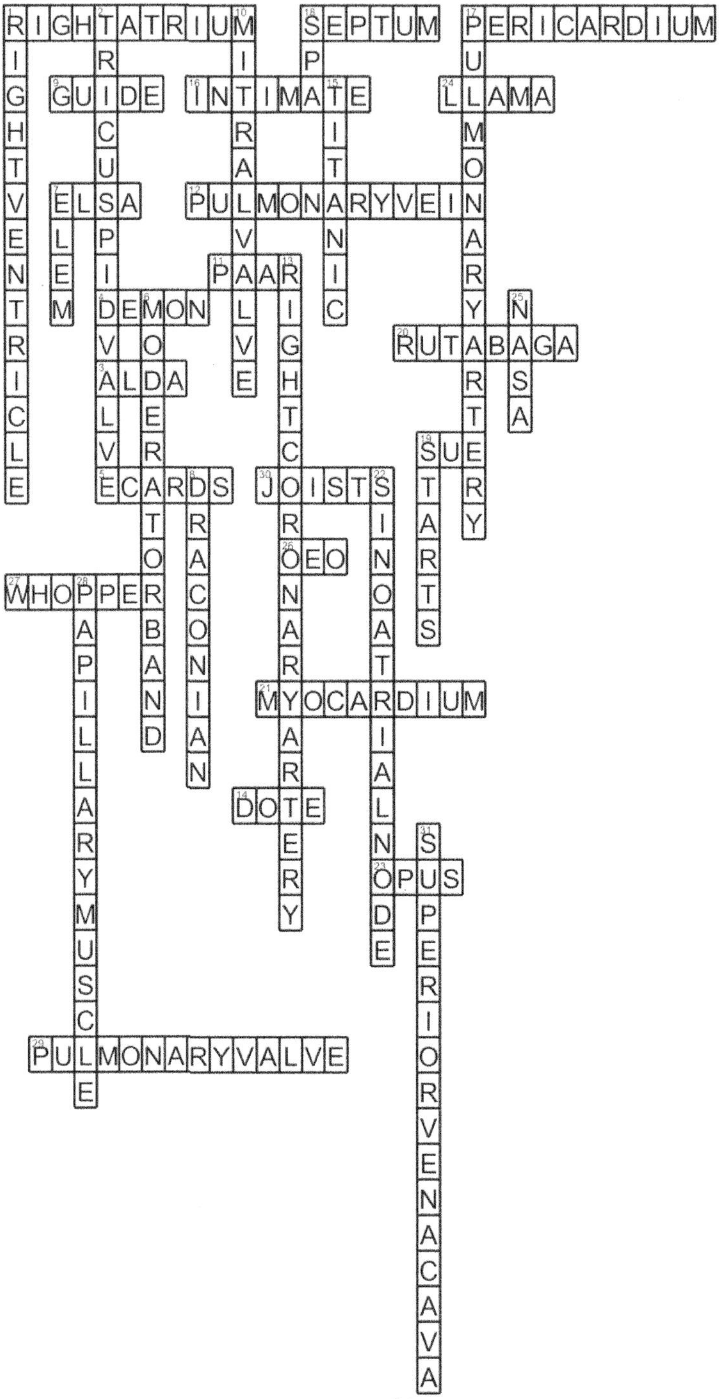

Cardiac Medications 2

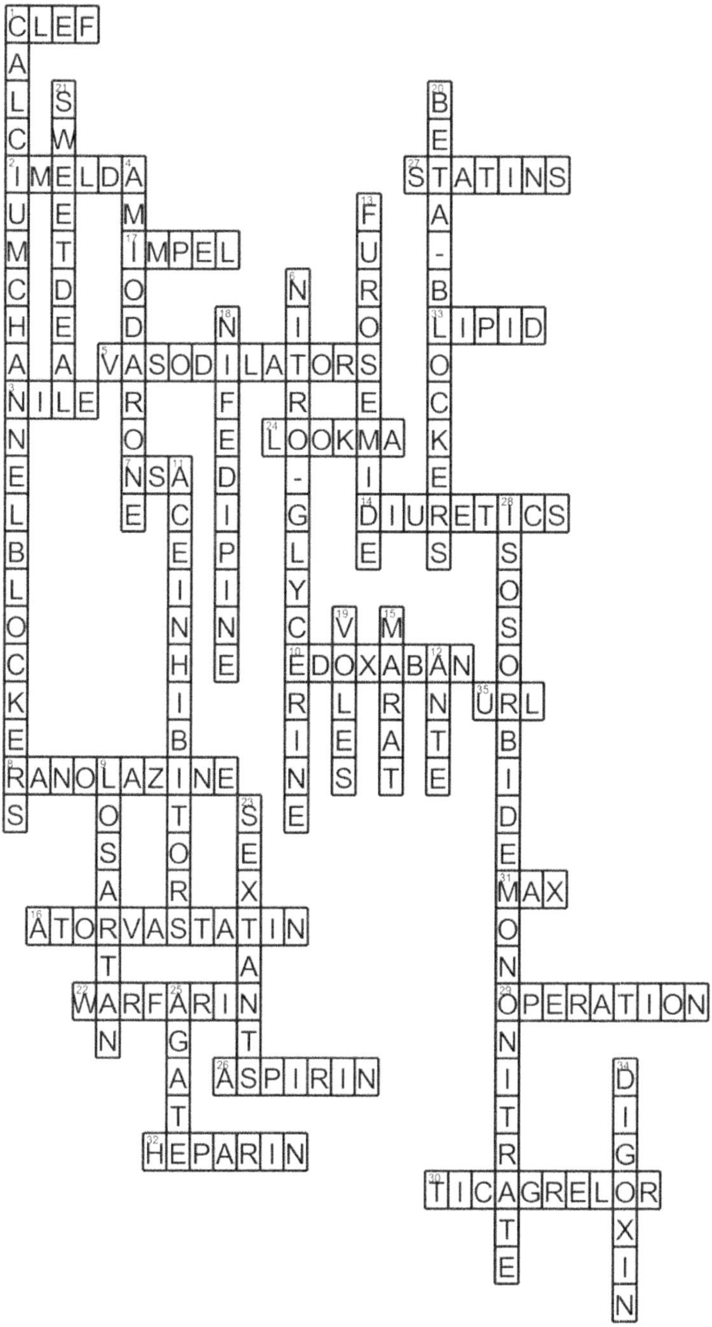

Investigations & Tests 2

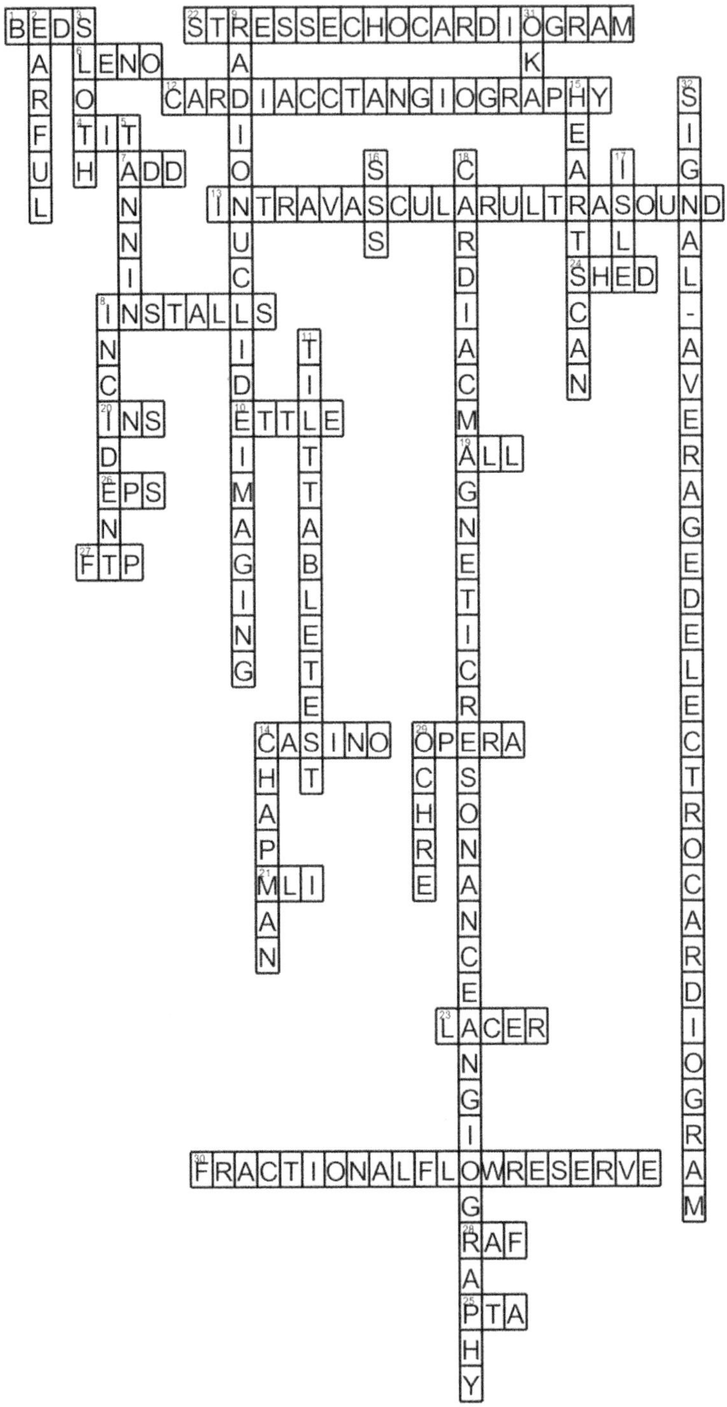

GRID - 1 (Solution)
Intermediate

6	5	3	4	8	2	9	1	7
4	7	1	9	3	6	8	2	5
9	8	2	1	5	7	3	4	6
8	3	7	6	2	1	5	9	4
1	6	5	8	9	4	7	3	2
2	9	4	5	7	3	6	8	1
5	4	9	2	6	8	1	7	3
7	2	8	3	1	5	4	6	9
3	1	6	7	4	9	2	5	8

GRID - 2 (Solution)
Intermediate

3	5	2	1	8	4	7	9	6
7	6	8	2	3	9	5	4	1
4	1	9	5	7	6	3	8	2
9	4	1	3	2	5	8	6	7
5	8	6	7	4	1	2	3	9
2	7	3	9	6	8	1	5	4
6	2	7	4	5	3	9	1	8
1	3	4	8	9	2	6	7	5
8	9	5	6	1	7	4	2	3

GRID - 3 (Solution)
Intermediate

6	4	3	5	1	9	8	7	2
8	5	7	6	4	2	9	1	3
2	9	1	7	3	8	4	6	5
9	3	8	2	6	5	1	4	7
1	6	4	3	9	7	5	2	8
5	7	2	4	8	1	3	9	6
4	2	6	1	5	3	7	8	9
3	1	9	8	7	6	2	5	4
7	8	5	9	2	4	6	3	1

GRID - 4 (Solution)
Intermediate

9	3	2	6	1	5	8	7	4
7	1	5	8	2	4	9	3	6
8	6	4	7	9	3	5	1	2
4	9	3	5	6	8	1	2	7
6	5	1	2	7	9	3	4	8
2	7	8	3	4	1	6	5	9
1	8	7	4	3	6	2	9	5
5	4	9	1	8	2	7	6	3
3	2	6	9	5	7	4	8	1

GRID - 5 (Solution)

Easy

2	3	8	4	1	5	9	7	6
4	7	6	9	3	2	5	8	1
5	1	9	6	7	8	4	2	3
9	6	7	1	2	3	8	4	5
1	8	2	7	5	4	3	6	9
3	5	4	8	9	6	7	1	2
6	9	3	2	8	7	1	5	4
8	4	1	5	6	9	2	3	7
7	2	5	3	4	1	6	9	8

GRID - 6 (Solution)

Easy

1	2	8	7	4	6	9	5	3
9	3	4	8	1	5	2	6	7
7	5	6	3	2	9	4	8	1
2	4	7	9	5	8	1	3	6
8	6	1	2	3	7	5	9	4
5	9	3	4	6	1	8	7	2
3	1	5	6	8	4	7	2	9
4	7	2	5	9	3	6	1	8
6	8	9	1	7	2	3	4	5

GRID - 7 (Solution)

Easy

4	8	2	7	5	3	6	9	1
7	5	6	9	2	1	4	8	3
9	3	1	6	4	8	7	5	2
8	9	3	5	7	6	1	2	4
6	4	5	2	1	9	8	3	7
2	1	7	3	8	4	5	6	9
1	2	8	4	3	5	9	7	6
5	7	9	1	6	2	3	4	8
3	6	4	8	9	7	2	1	5

GRID - 8 (Solution)

Easy

2	3	7	6	5	4	1	8	9
5	9	8	1	7	2	4	3	6
4	6	1	3	8	9	2	5	7
9	1	5	7	3	6	8	4	2
8	7	2	4	1	5	6	9	3
3	4	6	9	2	8	7	1	5
6	5	3	8	4	7	9	2	1
1	8	9	2	6	3	5	7	4
7	2	4	5	9	1	3	6	8

GRID - 1 (Solution)

Hard

9	8	6	7	1	4	3	2	5
5	7	2	3	6	8	4	1	9
1	4	3	5	2	9	8	7	6
7	1	8	9	3	2	6	5	4
2	3	4	8	5	6	7	9	1
6	9	5	1	4	7	2	8	3
3	5	7	6	8	1	9	4	2
8	2	1	4	9	3	5	6	7
4	6	9	2	7	5	1	3	8

GRID - 2 (Solution)

Hard

1	8	4	5	7	9	3	2	6
2	6	3	4	8	1	9	5	7
9	5	7	3	6	2	1	8	4
5	1	2	9	4	7	8	6	3
3	7	9	8	1	6	5	4	2
8	4	6	2	3	5	7	1	9
7	9	8	1	2	4	6	3	5
6	2	1	7	5	3	4	9	8
4	3	5	6	9	8	2	7	1

GRID - 3 (Solution)

Hard

3	4	5	2	7	8	6	1	9
6	1	7	9	5	3	8	2	4
2	8	9	1	6	4	5	3	7
8	7	6	5	9	1	3	4	2
5	9	1	3	4	2	7	8	6
4	2	3	6	8	7	9	5	1
1	6	8	7	2	5	4	9	3
9	5	2	4	3	6	1	7	8
7	3	4	8	1	9	2	6	5

GRID - 4 (Solution)

Hard

4	6	2	7	8	1	9	5	3
8	9	5	4	2	3	7	6	1
7	1	3	6	5	9	2	4	8
9	7	8	3	4	2	5	1	6
1	5	6	8	9	7	4	3	2
3	2	4	1	6	5	8	7	9
5	4	1	2	3	8	6	9	7
2	3	9	5	7	6	1	8	4
6	8	7	9	1	4	3	2	5

GRID - 5 (Solution)

Hard

7	1	9	6	4	3	8	5	2
2	4	8	7	9	5	6	1	3
6	3	5	8	1	2	7	4	9
1	7	3	9	2	8	4	6	5
4	8	2	1	5	6	9	3	7
5	9	6	3	7	4	1	2	8
9	6	1	5	3	7	2	8	4
8	5	4	2	6	9	3	7	1
3	2	7	4	8	1	5	9	6

GRID - 6 (Solution)

Hard

1	3	5	4	9	6	2	7	8
8	9	6	5	2	7	4	3	1
7	2	4	8	1	3	5	9	6
4	6	9	2	7	8	1	5	3
2	7	1	9	3	5	6	8	4
5	8	3	1	6	4	7	2	9
3	5	2	6	4	9	8	1	7
6	1	7	3	8	2	9	4	5
9	4	8	7	5	1	3	6	2

GRID - 7 (Solution)

Hard

7	1	8	5	4	9	2	3	6
9	4	5	6	2	3	1	8	7
6	2	3	1	8	7	4	5	9
2	9	7	4	6	5	8	1	3
3	8	1	7	9	2	5	6	4
5	6	4	8	3	1	7	9	2
4	5	2	3	1	6	9	7	8
1	3	9	2	7	8	6	4	5
8	7	6	9	5	4	3	2	1

GRID - 8 (Solution)

Hard

1	6	4	5	2	3	8	7	9
2	3	5	8	9	7	1	6	4
8	9	7	4	1	6	2	3	5
5	2	1	6	7	9	4	8	3
4	8	9	1	3	5	7	2	6
6	7	3	2	4	8	5	9	1
3	1	6	7	5	2	9	4	8
7	4	8	9	6	1	3	5	2
9	5	2	3	8	4	6	1	7

GRID - 1 (Solution)

Very Hard

7	6	4	8	9	5	3	1	2
5	3	8	6	1	2	7	9	4
1	2	9	3	4	7	8	5	6
3	1	6	7	5	9	4	2	8
2	8	5	1	3	4	6	7	9
4	9	7	2	8	6	1	3	5
6	4	1	5	2	3	9	8	7
8	7	2	9	6	1	5	4	3
9	5	3	4	7	8	2	6	1

GRID - 2 (Solution)

Very Hard

7	3	1	9	8	2	6	4	5
8	5	9	3	6	4	1	2	7
4	6	2	1	7	5	9	8	3
1	4	6	7	5	8	2	3	9
3	2	7	4	1	9	5	6	8
9	8	5	2	3	6	7	1	4
6	7	4	8	9	1	3	5	2
5	9	8	6	2	3	4	7	1
2	1	3	5	4	7	8	9	6

GRID - 3 (Solution)

Very Hard

3	7	1	9	8	2	6	5	4
2	8	4	7	6	5	1	9	3
6	5	9	3	4	1	8	2	7
7	4	3	5	1	9	2	6	8
1	9	2	6	3	8	7	4	5
8	6	5	4	2	7	9	3	1
4	2	6	1	7	3	5	8	9
9	1	8	2	5	4	3	7	6
5	3	7	8	9	6	4	1	2

GRID - 4 (Solution)

Very Hard

4	5	8	1	3	6	7	2	9
2	6	3	5	7	9	4	8	1
7	9	1	8	4	2	5	6	3
6	1	5	4	8	3	9	7	2
9	8	2	7	6	1	3	5	4
3	4	7	2	9	5	8	1	6
5	3	4	6	1	7	2	9	8
1	2	9	3	5	8	6	4	7
8	7	6	9	2	4	1	3	5

GRID - 1 (Solution)

Insane

3	2	9	4	1	5	6	8	7
1	8	4	2	6	7	9	3	5
7	5	6	8	9	3	1	2	4
9	3	1	6	7	4	8	5	2
5	6	8	3	2	1	4	7	9
2	4	7	5	8	9	3	1	6
4	7	5	9	3	8	2	6	1
6	9	3	1	5	2	7	4	8
8	1	2	7	4	6	5	9	3

GRID - 2 (Solution)

Insane

1	6	5	8	7	2	9	4	3
4	9	3	6	5	1	7	8	2
7	2	8	4	9	3	5	1	6
8	1	7	9	4	6	3	2	5
6	5	9	2	3	8	1	7	4
2	3	4	5	1	7	8	6	9
5	8	1	3	2	4	6	9	7
9	7	2	1	6	5	4	3	8
3	4	6	7	8	9	2	5	1

GRID - 3 (Solution)

Insane

7	3	8	4	5	6	2	9	1
6	1	5	7	9	2	4	8	3
4	9	2	8	3	1	7	6	5
5	4	7	6	1	9	3	2	8
3	2	6	5	7	8	9	1	4
9	8	1	3	2	4	6	5	7
1	5	4	9	6	7	8	3	2
8	6	3	2	4	5	1	7	9
2	7	9	1	8	3	5	4	6

GRID - 4 (Solution)

Insane

5	9	7	6	1	8	2	4	3
4	2	8	7	3	5	6	9	1
6	3	1	9	2	4	5	7	8
1	8	6	3	4	9	7	2	5
7	4	9	1	5	2	8	3	6
3	5	2	8	7	6	4	1	9
9	7	4	5	8	3	1	6	2
2	6	5	4	9	1	3	8	7
8	1	3	2	6	7	9	5	4

Heart Health Words & Phrases

Solution 1	**Solution 2**	**Solution 3**
Age	Weight Loss	Open Heart Surgery
STEMI	Cardiologist	Coronary Thrombosis
Stent	Healthy Diet	High Blood Pressure
Gender	Heart Attack	Silent Heart Attack
NSTEMI	Risk Factors	Occupational Therapy
Obesity	Family History	Myocardial Infarction
Smoking	Angina Pectoris	Sudden Cardiac Arrest
Asystole	Heart Transplant	Cardiac Rehabilitation
Diabetes	High Cholesterol	Coronary Artery Disease
Exercise	Physical Therapy	Ventricular Fibrillation
Angiogram	Electrocardiogram	Coronary Artery Bypass Grafting
Nutrition	Lifestyle Changes	Percutaneous Coronary Intervention
Pulseless	Smoking Cessation	
Medication	Stress Management	
Angioplasty	Valve Replacement	

Australian Hospitals (Solution)

OYALR LNEOBMRUE LPOHTAIS	Royal Melbourne Hospital
HTE RNIEPC ERSLACH ILPHTAOS	The Prince Charles Hospital
TS NT'NCSVIE OPSATILH	St Vincent's Hospital
AONSMH DAIMCEL CEERNT	Monash Medical Centre
NTISAU IHATPLOS RBIDGELEEH	Austin Hospital Heidelberg
HET ELARFD	The Alfred
NS'HDILREC IHLTPASO TA ETMSEADW	Children's Hospital at Westmead
TS TNNVI'CSE IEVTARP SPHOATLI STAE ORBUNLEEM	St Vincent's Private Hospital East Melbourne
OERPLVOIL TRAEH & TSCHE SPTAOHLI	Liverpool Heart & Chest Hospital
RLAYO NPCREI DRALFE OLATSIPH	Royal Prince Alfred Hospital
NYYEDS IAVSTTEND HPSATOLI	Sydney Adventist Hospital
WTESERN OAPHLITS	Western Hospital
TEH EELSWY ALITHOSP	The Wesley Hospital
ORAYL BBAENRSI & 'OSNWME IALPHOTS	Royal Brisbane & Women's Hospital
EDSTEWMA POSHILAT	Westmead Hospital

Canadian Hospitals (Solution)

RTNOOTO ALNEERG	Toronto General
ONETMRLA EAGERNL PSTIAOLH	Montreal General Hospital
MNOUT AINSI LPSTHAOI	Mount Sinai Hospital
YNROUNKSOB LEHHAT CNESCISE TERNCE	Sunnybrook Health Sciences Centre
RVVEUACON ANLEGRE HPTAOLSI	Vancouver General Hospital
TS MLH'SEAIC OISHAPLT	St Michael's Hospital
ERETNC IALOHIPETSR ED VNRSIUTEÉL'I ED MNATOLÉR	Centre hospitalier de l'Université de Montréal
EHWSIJ EREANLG PALITSOH	Jewish General Hospital
GCMLLI TIENIYRSVU AHTHEL EERTNC	McGill University Health Centre
NTHRO ORKY LNERGAE APILTSHO	North York General Hospital
AOYLR IJEBEUL HPLAIOTS	Royal Jubilee Hospital
S.T AULSP' AILOTPSH	St. Paul's Hospital

UK Hospitals (Solution)

RLOAY MPTRBOON SLTHIOAP	Royal Brompton Hospital
RGATE OMRODN SREETT HSTLIPOA	Great Ormond Street Hospital
NHJO CAFEFLRID HASTPILO	John Radcliffe Hospital
'SKNIG GECLOLE OHPSLAIT	King's College Hospital
YLARO TRHWPPOA IPALSHTO	Royal Papworth Hospital
.ST BOMTERWHLA'OS OHISTAPL	St. Bartholomew's Hospital
RLFEIAHED ATIOSHLP	Harefield Hospital
LEOOVIPLR EAHTR DNA TSHEC STOPLHIA	Liverpool Heart and Chest Hospital
YU'GS LOAPIHTS	Guy's Hospital
RAHICNG SCSRO OAPISTLH	Charing Cross Hospital
TS O'AHSTM SLOTPIHA	St Thomas' Hospital
BADDKR'OSEENO	Addenbrooke's
YSAWNTHEEHW IOHTSLPA	Wythenshawe Hospital
MIEMSMHAHRT HOTSLIPA	Hammersmith Hospital
AYRLO EERF HPTSIOAL	Royal Free Hospital
NODGLE JIUEELB ANOTNALI IALSTPOH	Golden Jubilee National Hospital
RYOAL RYMNFIRIA FO RUIENGHDB TA LLTIET REFANC	Royal Infirmary of Edinburgh at Little France
DORIRDREF PATLSOHI	Derriford Hospital

US Hospitals (Solution)

VNLALDCEE ILICCN	Cleveland Clinic
OYMA LICNCI	Mayo Clinic
EHTTCAASSUSMS RNLGAEE PALTSHIO	Massachusetts General Hospital
TEH HOSJN HKOINPS OLPTHIAS	The Johns Hopkins Hospital
HTE UTOMN NISIA LSPHOAIT	The Mount Sinai Hospital
ARHIBMG DNA NME'OSW HPAISLTO	Brigham And Women's Hospital
ENW YOKR ESBPTINRAYER HISOPALT	New York Presbyterian Hospital
LABORY TS E'UKSL MACELID CNREET	Baylor St Luke's Medical Center
DRSECA NIAIS EALDMIC CNTEER	Cedars Sinai Medical Center
OFRSANTD ITLSAPHO	Stanford Hospital
UNY NOALEGN IOPSTLAHS	NYU Langone Hospitals
UEDK TIVNYSUIRE AIPSOTLH	Duke University Hospital
ULCA EHHTAL – ONLRAD GRNEAA LMCDAIE ENRETC	UCLA Health – Ronald Reagan Medical Center
NTNEERTRHSWO MLOREIMA HILATPSO	Northwestern Memorial Hospital
HIPASTLO FO ETH TENSRIIVYU FO EYSAPLNNNAIV	Hospital of the University of Pennsylvania
TONOUSH MSHOETTID HPOSLITA	Houston Methodist Hospital
IVRNUIESYT FO AICCOHG MCELAID ETRCEN	University of Chicago Medical Center
NOBOTS LRNESICHD ISAOLHTP	Boston Childrens Hospital
USFC LAEICMD RCTNEE	UCSF Medical Center
IIRNTYSVEU FO INICGMHA ISAOPHLT	University of Michigan Hospital

WORDS OF WELLBEING 1 (Solution)

J	N	R	F	M	L	V	X	Y	T	D	T	W	N	J	E	I	T	W	D
V	X	B	I	T	A	M	M	E	C	K	S	Z	O	X	H	Z	J	T	F
T	A	X	C	X	G	I	F	J	G	N	E	X	E	R	B	G	G	M	Z
X	W	E	K	L	O	D	P	T	N	B	R	R	I	I	K	E	O	J	N
R	E	K	A	M	M	V	P	R	M	A	C	N	B	O	T	O	M	Y	T
N	L	A	W	E	T	T	M	M	E	I	C	K	A	H	Z	K	U	T	A
T	L	T	S	P	Z	Y	G	E	S	D	H	R	F	L	W	W	G	T	H
M	N	N	Y	A	P	N	N	E	C	L	O	E	D	P	T	N	B	I	I
E	E	I	B	T	W	S	U	O	W	K	Z	L	T	E	O	B	A	L	E
Q	S	R	G	D	I	E	K	T	I	D	I	A	G	P	E	E	L	S	M
C	S	E	C	Z	R	V	C	Q	R	T	K	X	S	H	R	K	M	A	T
S	P	T	Z	Y	H	T	I	D	H	I	A	A	F	L	N	W	N	D	F
M	S	A	P	C	L	W	D	T	P	L	T	T	F	Y	I	I	O	E	B
X	S	W	X	K	R	R	E	O	C	B	A	I	I	L	V	Q	I	H	A
F	I	T	N	E	S	S	E	K	A	A	I	O	O	D	G	M	T	Z	C
Z	R	C	S	R	D	X	C	Y	A	D	T	N	Z	N	E	W	A	C	B
P	A	L	G	D	L	V	I	L	W	A	K	H	Y	Z	P	M	R	Z	I
D	E	Q	G	N	I	T	A	E	Y	H	T	L	A	E	H	V	D	W	V
X	G	S	T	N	E	M	E	L	P	P	U	S	L	Y	M	T	Y	T	I
O	C	E	M	V	Q	V	I	T	A	M	I	N	S	H	A	E	H	K	A

WORDS OF WELLBEING 2 (Solution)

Y	P	W	Y	X	I	J	K	W	X	E	M	B	S	A	Q	W	C	H	B
T	R	R	Q	S	K	G	K	Y	T	I	L	I	B	I	X	E	L	F	E
E	I	M	M	U	N	I	T	Y	N	F	D	N	Q	H	T	L	A	E	H
C	S	N	R	P	B	S	K	H	O	M	E	G	B	K	Q	F	F	E	V
N	C	L	E	A	N	S	I	N	G	G	T	S	Z	D	X	F	E	I	P
A	H	G	C	C	N	L	Y	H	W	Z	O	X	I	B	K	W	Y	O	G
L	C	T	O	I	K	W	C	I	X	L	X	R	R	Q	T	K	G	K	O
A	H	G	V	Q	P	R	E	V	E	N	T	I	O	N	S	T	P	I	J
B	D	Y	E	P	Q	E	Y	N	R	Y	O	I	H	O	W	H	V	T	G
Z	F	E	R	O	P	O	G	T	C	N	M	Y	T	E	I	X	N	A	A
K	X	T	Y	R	X	C	M	Y	I	R	X	G	C	V	V	K	W	Y	H
I	Z	N	S	T	S	V	D	J	M	L	O	H	H	Q	S	T	P	I	E
J	G	A	Q	R	I	Q	S	A	Y	S	I	P	W	H	H	X	E	F	A
E	C	N	A	T	S	I	S	E	R	W	T	B	C	H	W	B	R	B	L
J	F	Q	A	V	O	I	D	A	N	C	E	R	A	G	T	K	Q	T	I
R	X	D	M	S	T	Y	J	F	W	X	G	K	E	T	V	Z	T	H	N
F	F	E	Q	U	I	L	I	B	R	I	U	M	D	S	P	H	G	K	G
P	Y	K	J	S	M	N	J	X	K	E	A	Q	K	W	S	A	S	M	V
A	R	R	J	J	Z	O	H	X	F	X	G	R	Y	R	C	I	D	K	H
V	L	S	V	S	Z	F	G	S	T	Y	J	E	Q	Z	N	R	I	A	D

WORDS OF WELLBEING 3 (Solution)

A	C	C	Q	G	N	I	N	A	E	M	Q	W	F	Y	L	V	L	P	Z
C	O	Y	M	K	K	K	M	D	I	D	V	P	G	Q	L	N	J	X	K
C	A	S	Q	J	V	Q	K	S	Y	N	O	I	T	C	E	N	N	O	C
E	N	N	G	O	Q	I	G	P	D	N	G	J	X	Q	P	L	W	T	C
P	Q	R	V	S	Y	A	F	R	S	Y	I	A	N	X	D	P	Z	X	S
T	G	E	M	M	L	P	F	B	G	X	O	O	K	M	N	J	X	D	I
A	V	D	K	L	X	K	E	N	D	U	R	A	N	C	E	M	T	Z	H
N	Q	U	J	F	O	R	T	I	T	U	D	E	O	Q	B	O	R	G	Q
C	H	T	K	A	N	I	M	A	T	S	Z	K	R	N	Y	M	W	F	S
E	B	I	P	M	S	I	I	L	D	K	X	V	H	J	E	E	J	M	R
L	L	T	J	N	P	N	Q	I	D	H	Z	C	C	N	L	N	Q	L	Z
F	O	A	B	W	L	N	Z	L	N	W	T	K	T	S	C	C	S	Z	C
S	V	R	O	S	B	M	A	M	S	P	Z	A	Q	I	T	Z	Q	P	V
O	E	G	J	N	P	T	D	O	R	S	L	H	L	Y	I	X	L	J	J
H	K	P	H	Y	S	I	C	A	L	B	L	A	N	O	I	T	O	M	E
F	K	V	G	G	Q	E	G	A	R	U	O	C	K	L	G	V	H	L	K
I	X	F	I	K	S	Y	N	N	G	G	W	A	D	V	B	T	D	O	H
O	I	Z	G	F	S	R	E	S	I	L	I	E	N	C	E	J	P	S	Q
X	C	F	R	E	S	O	P	R	U	P	S	X	H	A	N	W	L	P	Z
M	S	I	M	I	T	P	O	O	Y	M	L	M	L	N	F	B	F	X	J

WORDS OF WELLBEING 4 (Solution)

H	I	J	K	M	H	W	B	J	A	R	P	H	T	P	L	S	Y	P	S
P	H	I	P	E	F	N	O	C	M	E	R	A	C	F	L	E	S	P	E
F	H	C	Y	R	Q	M	U	X	V	D	R	O	T	D	B	J	K	L	L
G	T	R	S	T	Y	O	N	A	P	X	D	N	M	Q	A	X	R	A	F
N	G	E	L	L	M	P	D	G	C	G	E	Y	L	B	B	K	M	Y	A
I	N	A	J	X	C	O	A	V	K	M	M	X	A	J	O	Y	D	F	W
H	G	T	P	V	C	K	R	C	T	Z	L	B	C	B	R	G	R	U	A
S	J	I	L	Z	L	R	I	N	N	Y	X	G	F	T	P	M	T	L	R
I	I	V	H	V	N	S	E	C	N	A	D	N	U	B	A	C	I	N	E
R	Q	I	T	H	T	T	S	X	E	W	K	P	P	P	R	O	D	E	N
U	J	T	E	F	N	F	P	Q	S	N	E	G	B	X	M	N	Z	S	E
O	N	Y	R	O	Y	X	M	V	F	F	V	Z	C	T	O	F	T	S	S
L	O	P	C	O	G	C	N	D	R	R	X	A	Y	X	C	M	Q	R	S
F	X	Y	H	T	A	P	M	E	G	C	V	V	K	N	Y	B	Z	N	L
L	K	N	D	J	P	G	R	A	C	E	M	W	H	H	S	M	N	J	X
K	E	A	Q	E	K	W	Q	L	F	L	B	B	Y	Y	K	P	W	J	T
H	W	B	A	L	D	C	I	K	H	V	L	R	V	S	Z	F	H	V	V
A	K	C	I	N	O	I	S	S	A	P	M	O	C	F	L	E	S	Q	Z
N	E	R	I	D	I	R	P	P	T	N	E	M	L	L	I	F	L	U	F
N	R	J	D	J	Z	L	C	M	Z	E	X	H	Y	L	C	O	X	F	I

WORDS OF WELLBEING 5 (Solution)

P	Z	G	M	S	I	A	V	Z	O	B	O	C	Y	V	Y	M	T	S	E
E	O	D	I	I	N	M	W	S	J	E	I	L	E	J	J	R	Q	E	G
A	I	N	V	G	N	T	A	S	F	T	Y	D	E	O	O	Q	O	H	H
C	D	I	P	M	Z	D	J	S	R	W	L	C	J	Y	L	N	Z	O	S
E	Y	M	Y	V	H	B	F	A	S	T	B	E	C	F	A	H	N	M	M
F	G	A	J	W	S	W	N	U	P	A	K	L	L	U	T	E	N	Q	L
U	T	T	E	X	P	Q	D	R	L	F	G	R	D	L	Y	G	P	M	C
L	A	I	D	D	U	T	O	Y	B	N	R	E	I	N	R	O	L	A	V
N	E	V	Y	I	F	T	Z	J	I	F	E	J	G	E	M	X	C	H	J
E	N	E	L	Y	E	L	M	B	F	Q	W	S	Q	S	F	B	C	B	D
S	D	I	Z	I	I	D	N	Q	P	Y	S	V	S	S	Q	O	Q	E	D
S	T	C	N	X	Q	I	Y	S	A	C	X	X	P	Q	B	G	T	E	N
Y	B	M	I	N	S	P	I	R	A	T	I	O	N	O	P	O	P	Y	S
L	K	G	R	P	N	D	L	N	M	S	E	I	L	M	X	O	R	B	H
Y	C	W	Z	G	L	F	X	V	V	W	Z	Q	M	Q	H	D	T	L	V
W	Y	T	F	W	K	O	E	W	D	E	X	O	G	I	E	V	N	I	M
T	A	R	A	S	V	X	Q	P	Z	E	N	L	W	T	C	Q	I	C	C
K	C	M	Y	Z	O	G	C	Y	T	I	N	A	S	T	I	K	W	C	J
C	W	A	A	Z	I	N	A	I	R	A	T	E	G	E	V	V	Q	V	H
R	R	Z	E	O	Z	K	S	N	F	Y	M	Y	A	G	O	Y	L	N	W

ABOUT THE AUTHOR

Sallie Crawley has over 17 years' experience as a coach and therapist. She is a certified Life Coach and ILM Executive Coach and Mentor. She is also certified as a Master Practitioner of Neuro Linguistic Programming and trained as a Clinical Hypnotherapist.

Since overcoming breast cancer and surviving a heart attack, she specialises in helping people who have had a heart attack learn to live life and love life again. She helps with anxiety, panic, sleeplessness, creating the mind-set to make exercise & dietary changes, relaxation, smoking cessation and confidence.

As a North Londoner, her career was originally in the print and communications industry. Spending some 16 years she gained experience working in commercial, report and accounts and food labelling printing companies. She managed teams in admin, production and sales.

After a year out to be a full-time mum and a move to a small village, Sallie had a career change. In 2002 she joined the RSPB (UK conservation charity) as the HQ Volunteering Operations Team Manager. Her team supported volunteers throughout the UK for 17 years and was inspired and proud of the contribution that the 12,000+ volunteers made to the cause.

Sallie also proudly volunteers as a Trustee of a local charity, the Hunts Cancer Community Network. Empowering people to take control of their diagnosis and take an active part in managing their health and wellbeing.

She lives in Cambridgeshire, UK with her daughter, their dogs, two cats and a fish called Lonely.

OTHER BOOKS ON AMAZON BY SALLIE

Sallie has also written other books to support you with the practical and emotional side of life when living with heart disease and recovering from a heart attack or heart surgery. They're available on Amazon and are called *The Beat Goes On* and *Beyond the Beat*.

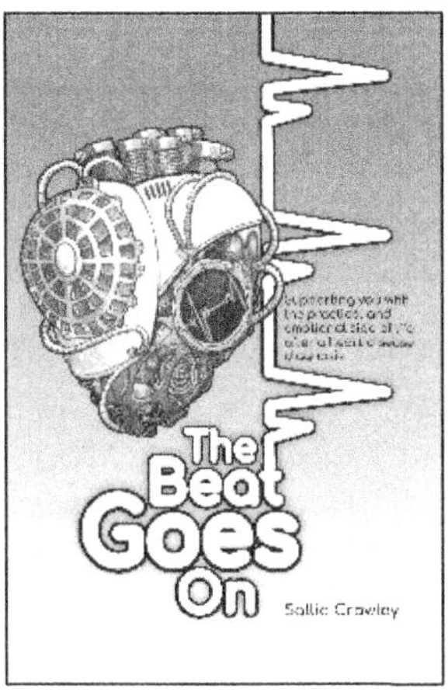

The Beat Goes On - Supporting you with the practical and emotional side of life when living with heart disease when you're first diagnosed.

UK https://amzn.to/4bwWgxz
US www.amazon.com
AU www.amazon.com.au
CA www.amazon.ca

Beyond The Beat - Your guide for before and after heart surgery or a heart attack for emotional resilience. Taking back your life with actionable steps.

UK https://amzn.to/4bpZwei
US www.amazon.com
AU www.amazon.com.au
CA www.amazon.ca

Printed in Great Britain
by Amazon

51903246R00066